BIOMES AND ECOSYSTEMS

THE LIVING EARTH

BIOMES AND ECOSYSTEMS

EDITED BY JOHN P. RAFFERTY, ASSOCIATE EDITOR, EARTH AND LIFE SCIENCES

Britannica®
Educational Publishing

IN ASSOCIATION WITH

ROSEN
EDUCATIONAL SERVICES

Published in 2011 by Britannica Educational Publishing
(a trademark of Encyclopædia Britannica, Inc.)
in association with Rosen Educational Services, LLC
29 East 21st Street, New York, NY 10010.

First Edition

Britannica Educational Publishing
Michael I. Levy: Executive Editor
J.E. Luebering: Senior Manager
Marilyn L. Barton: Senior Coordinator, Production Control
Steven Bosco: Director, Editorial Technologies
Lisa S. Braucher: Senior Producer and Data Editor
Yvette Charboneau: Senior Copy Editor
Kathy Nakamura: Manager, Media Acquisition
John P. Rafferty: Associate Editor, Earth and Life Sciences

Rosen Educational Services
Jeanne Nagle: Senior Editor
Nelson Sá: Art Director
Cindy Reiman: Photography Manager
Matthew Cauli: Designer, Cover Design
Introduction by Jeanne Nagle

Library of Congress Cataloging-in-Publication Data

Biomes and ecosystems / edited by John P. Rafferty. — 1st ed.
    p. cm. -- (The living earth)
"In association with Britannica Educational Publishing, Rosen Educational Services."
Includes bibliographical references and index.
ISBN 978-1-61530-302-1 (library binding)
1. Biotic communities—Juvenile literature. 2. Ecology—Juvenile literature.
3. Evolution (Biology)—Juvenile literature. I. Rafferty, John P.
QH541.14.B56 2011
577—dc22

2010015407

Manufactured in the United States of America

On the cover: A bee gathers nectar from the flower of a catnip plant. Interdependence and
biodiversity are keys to the survival of the world's biomes and ecosystems. *Hope Lourie Killcoyne*

On page x: A rainbow arches over the rainforest in Malaysia. Though defined by diverse
biota and climates, Earth's biomes and ecosystems share one common element—majestic,
natural beauty. *AFP/Getty Images*

On pages v, 1, 38, 69, 104, 136, 199, 201, 209: A view of Scout Lake in Deschutes National
Park, Oregon, with Mount Jefferson in the background. *Erik Hovmiller Photography/Flickr/
Getty Images*

CONTENTS

5

28

34

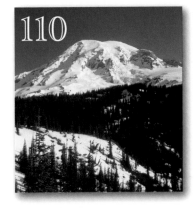

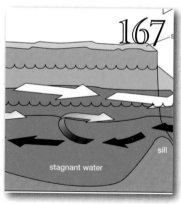

INTRODUCTION

Outside of a zoo or perhaps a traveling circus, you wouldn't expect to encounter an elephant in the urban wilds of a North American or European city. Likewise, palm trees don't sprout in Alaska, nor do fresh-water fish abound in the saline waters of the world's oceans. That's because the environmental conditions in one region of the planet are not conducive to all life-forms. Every living thing on Earth has a specific place to call home, geographic areas that scientists have grouped into life zones called biomes and ecosystems. This book explains these concepts in detail, as well as the ways in which life is created and sustained, how living organisms and their nonliving surroundings keep nature in balance, and the importance of maintaining a healthy diversity among Earth's creatures and their habitats.

Scientifically speaking, life is something of a top-down proposition. At the uppermost level is the biosphere, which is the part of the Earth system that supports life. The biosphere wends its way down to less sizeable components, including biomes and ecosystems. Each biome is a vast region of the planet that is home to similar types of plants and animals, which have adapted to said region's climate. In general, ecosystems are similar to biomes, but abiotic, or nonliving, elements also help to define them. Smaller units within the biosphere include communities and habitats.

The study of Earth's biomes and ecosystems begins with an investigation into the biosphere itself. Thin only in relation to the Earth's diameter, the biosphere covers the entire planetary surface, reaching up into the the atmosphere and down into the soil and rock beneath Earth's surface. This stratum's life-giving properties are powered by radiant energy from the Sun. Plants and other plantlike organisms soak up this energy and convert it to chemical energy, chiefly carbohydrates, through photo-synthesis. The flow of energy is passed through the food chain as plants are consumed by herbivores, which are in turn consumed by meat-eaters. At each link in the chain, energy potency is diluted. The majority of energy stored in plant matter never makes it into the food chain, however. It decays to form the soil upon which plants grow.

Energy is not the only thing passed along in the bio-sphere. A number of key nutrients necessary for cell growth are cycled through plants, animals, and the smaller organisms that break each living thing down after it dies. The six major nutrients thus cycled are hydrogen, oxygen, carbon, nitrogen, sulfur, and phosphorus. Changes to any one nutrient cycle can significantly alter the ability of plants and animals—even humans—to survive and reproduce.

As the biosphere has evolved over billions of years, so, too, have the life-forms it sustains. Over time, each has affected the other. For example, sea-dwelling bacteria, the earliest known life-forms on Earth, obtained nutrients from an atmosphere made up of significantly higher concentrations of carbon dioxide than today. Some bacteria acquired the ability to metabolize carbon dioxide and give off oxygen as a by-product. After vast amounts of carbon dioxide had been processed by these organisms, oxygen flooded the atmosphere, paving the way for the expansion of the biosphere and the evolution of creatures that could live on the land. Severe fluctuations in temperature such as those that occur during an ice age, changes to the dis-solved oxygen content in the seas, and other climatic or ecological events have necessitated that the flora and fauna of any given time either adapt or risk extinction. Natural occurrences, such as fire or volcanic activity, and the actions of humans—including over-hunting or -fishing and encroachment on feeding territories for housing and development—also have played a role in the evolution or extinction of certain species of plants and animals.

To more efficiently study and better understand the biosphere, scientists have divided it into more manageable portions. Parsing Earth's biosphere into regions defined by the plants and animals—referred to collectively as biota—that inhabit them is a concept known as biogeography. Identifying biogeographic regions in this manner dates back to the mid-1800s; research in this field had a hand in Charles Darwin's groundbreaking work on evolution. At one time biogeographic regions were based solely on boundaries suggested by endemic biota, which are animals and plants known to exist in only a limited area. Nowadays, however, there are formulas that take into account variances in species range, thereby mathematically deducing overall similarities in a region.

The distribution of a biogeographic region's plants (flora) is broken down into kingdoms, while animals (fauna) belong to realms. The six floral kingdoms and their various subkingdoms roughly coincide with the three primary faunal realms in terms of distinctiveness. In other words, biogeographic regions almost always contain endemic biota from overlapping floral kingdoms and faunal realms. The southern tip of South Africa, the Cape region, is the sole exception to this general rule. Animals on the Cape are not endemic to the region, but rather are part of a realm that encompasses Africa in its entirety. Only the rich, unique plant life in this area is differentiated enough so as to have warranted its own kingdom designation—the Capensic kingdom.

Within biogeographic regions are units known as biomes. The territory encompassed by each biome experiences a similar range of climactic conditions throughout, contains similar geologic features, and is home to several species of biota that are capable of surviving and reproducing in that space and under those particular conditions. Biomes can be either terrestrial or aquatic.

Because the biota in a biome are in such close proximity to each other and interact on a regular basis, the complex of organisms is often referred to as a biological community. Much like communities with human populations, biological communities consist of a variety of inhabitants that share living space in a delimited area. Each group also exhibits a propensity to band together when faced with adversity from other communities or natural disasters, and regroup once the threat has passed. The relationship between the inhabitants of biological communities and their biome environment is quite symbiotic. A change in climate can alter the evolution of species. Likewise, the extinction or removal of species can disrupt food chains and even weather patterns. This mutual dependency underscores the importance of biodiversity. Boiled down to its simplified essence, life on Earth is a group dynamic sustained by diverse individual entities. Simpler still is the notion that each living—and nonliving—thing plays an integral part in the survival of the planet. Without enough biodiversity, nutrient cycles become interrupted, ecological systems break down, and the complexion of biomes changes.

In the scientific vernacular, the terms "biome" and "ecosystem" have become interchangeable. Yet there is a difference between the two. Biomes are designated based primarily on the biota of an area and are smaller than ecosystems, which also consider a region's nonliving objects such as soil, water, and minerals. Ecosystems cut across a range of scales. Unique ecosystems can occur within separate drops of water, within different parts of a landscape (such as a single tree or stand of trees), between one landscape and another, or across vast regions such as continents. In fact, the biosphere is often referred to as a global ecosystem.

Seeking to better understand how life on Earth functions, scientists have noted the physical and biological activities that occur within each ecosystem, and the patterns that emerge among similar ecosystems separated by great distances. For instance, research into the climates and endemic biota of separate mountain ranges around the world has yielded information about mountain ecosystems in general. Mountain highlands support a healthy number of biological communities, although plant and animal populations are more scattered than they are in lowland ecosystems. Also, the greater the elevation, the fewer species there are in residence due to the harsh conditions found on and near mountain peaks.

Mountain ecosystems feature similar vegetation patterns: trees on the lower slopes and shorter, hearty alpine vegetation above. Tree growth ceases abruptly at the "tree line," marking where the growth areas switch dominance. Even though the specific type of tree that grows on mountain ranges varies, each mountain ecosystem has a tree line, and the vegetation there shows a high degree of biodiversity, since some species below the tree line and some species above meet each other in this location. In mountain ecosystems in general, conifers such as pine and spruces occur on northern temperate mountain ranges, whereas deciduous (broad-leafed) trees inhabit southern temperate slopes, and a mélange best described as "evergreen rainforest" in tropical locales. Mountain fauna consists primarily of species from surrounding lowland ecosystems that have adapted to live in mountain climates.

Careful examination of marine ecosystems through the years has led scientists to better understand and define the shape and depth of the world's oceans. Scientists have also gathered information on the intricate food chains at the pelagic level, a region of the ocean which encompasses virtually all the life in the ecosystem minus the biota that call the benthos (deep water and shelf) home. The individual food chains of coastal ecosystems are so interconnected they create what is called a food web, where multiple chains intersect in such a way as to form a vast feeding network. The availability of plankton, which is a primary food source in the marine ecosystem, is subject to seasonal patterns—somewhat analogous to fruits and vegetables being seasonally available in the human realm. Planktonic communities are made up of phytoplankton (which are photosynthetic) and zooplankton (which are not). Ocean currents, the amount of sunlight that reaches a particular aquatic life zone, and the reproductive cycles of plankton also affect food availability and the various forms of life in the marine ecosystem.

Scientists also study the relationships between one ecosystem and another. Unlike the demarcations that create states or provinces on the contiguous land of nations, biogeographic boundaries are not particularly cut and dried. Ecosystems that abut each other may experience some overlap. Such overlapping areas are called ecotones. In fact, one type of ecosystem is actually defined by the transitional zones between land and water ecosystems. Estuaries and lagoons, formed when one body of water meets another, are considered boundary ecosystems.

Plants are large and plentiful in boundary ecosystems. A combination of nutrients drawn from the two ecosystems occurs in these transition areas. Compared to the dark interiors of forests and the oceans, boundary ecosystems are characterized by increased sunlight and are thus more productive. Additional sunlight powers more photosynthetic activity. As a result, more energy is available for plant growth at the forest edge as well as in the shallow waters of lagoons, estuaries, and wetlands. In boundary ecosystems, while the plants benefit from increased sunlight, the animals that depend on them benefit from increased plant productivity.

Wetlands are particularly unique among this grouping, and appropriately named, because they are neither terrestrial nor aquatic, but rather a bit of both. These ecosystems may be more commonly known by their specific names: swamps, bogs, and marshes. The plants and animals that dwell in wetlands have adapted to living in an environment with perpetually saturated-to-flooded soil.

In an ever-changing world, the ability to adapt and adjust is key to survival. Over hundreds of millions of years, Earth has been altered by episodes of extreme climate change, the evolution of species, and natural disasters. Nevertheless, a diverse assemblage of modern species and ecosystems has arisen that interact with one another to form complex associations. These associations transfer energy and cycle nutrients to create the bountiful tapestry of life on Earth. Although Earth's biosphere faces threats from human activities, such as overdevelopment and pollution, life, in all its forms, is not so easily dissuaded. The existence, and perpetuation, of the world's biomes and ecosystems throughout geologic time is proof of that.

CHAPTER 1
EARTH'S BIOSPHERE

Before the coming of life, the Earth was a bleak place, a rocky globe with shallow seas and a thin band of gases—largely carbon dioxide, carbon monoxide, molecular nitrogen, hydrogen sulfide, and water vapour. It was a hostile and barren planet. This strictly inorganic state of the Earth is called the geosphere; it consists of the lithosphere (the rock and soil), the hydrosphere (the water), and the atmosphere (the air). Energy from the Sun relentlessly bombarded the surface of the primitive Earth, and in time—millions of years—chemical and physical actions produced the first evidence of life: formless, jellylike blobs that could collect energy from the environment and produce more of their own kind. This generation of life in the thin outer layer of the geosphere established what is called the biosphere, the "zone of life," an energy-diverting skin that uses the matter of the Earth to make living substance.

The biosphere is a system characterized by the continuous cycling of matter and an accompanying flow of solar energy in which certain large molecules and cells are self-reproducing. Water is a major predisposing factor, for all life depends on it. The elements carbon, hydrogen, nitrogen, oxygen, phosphorus, and sulfur, when combined as proteins, lipids, carbohydrates, and nucleic acids, provide the building blocks, the fuel, and the direction for the creation of life. Energy flow is required to maintain the structure of organisms by the formation and splitting of phosphate bonds. Organisms are cellular in nature and always contain some sort of enclosing membrane structure, and all have nucleic acids that store and transmit genetic information.

All life on Earth depends ultimately upon green plants, as well as upon water. Plants utilize sunlight in a

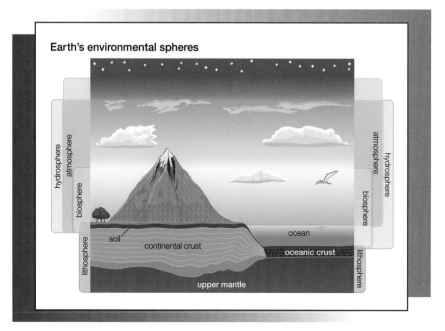

Earth's environmental spheres

Encyclopædia Britannica, Inc.

process called photosynthesis to produce the food upon which animals feed and to provide, as a by-product, oxygen, which most animals require for respiration. At first, the oceans and the lands were teeming with large numbers of a few kinds of simple single-celled organisms, but slowly plants and animals of increasing complexity evolved. Interrelationships developed so that certain plants grew in association with certain other plants, and animals associated with the plants and with one another to form communities of organisms, including those of forests, grasslands, deserts, dunes, bogs, rivers, and lakes. Living communities and their nonliving environment are inseparably interrelated and constantly interact upon each other. For convenience, any segment of the landscape that includes the biotic and abiotic components is called an ecosystem. A lake is an ecosystem when it is considered in totality as not just water but also nutrients, climate, and all of the life contained within it. A given forest, meadow, or river is likewise an ecosystem. One ecosystem grades into another along zones termed ecotones, where a mixture of plant and animal species from the two ecosystems occurs. A forest considered as an ecosystem is not simply a stand of trees but is a complex of soil, air, and water, of climate and minerals, of bacteria, viruses, fungi, grasses, herbs, and trees, of insects, reptiles, amphibians, birds, and mammals.

Stated another way, the abiotic, or nonliving, portion of each ecosystem in the biosphere includes the flow of energy, nutrients, water, and gases and the concentrations of organic and inorganic substances in the environment. The biotic, or living, portion includes three general categories of organisms based on their methods of acquiring energy: the primary producers, largely green plants; the consumers, which include all the animals; and the decomposers, which include the microorganisms that break down the remains of plants and animals into simpler components for recycling in the biosphere. Aquatic ecosystems are those involving marine environments and freshwater environments on the land. Terrestrial ecosystems are those based on major vegetational types, such as forest, grassland, desert, and tundra. Particular kinds of animals are associated with each such plant province.

Ecosystems may be further subdivided into smaller biotic units called communities. Examples of communities include the organisms in a stand of pine trees, on a coral reef, and in a cave, a valley, a lake, or a stream. The major consideration in the community is the living component, the organisms; the abiotic factors of the environment are excluded.

A community is a collection of species populations. In a stand of pines, there may be many species of insects, of birds, of mammals, each a separate breeding unit but each dependent on the others for its continued existence. A species, furthermore, is composed of individuals, single functioning units identifiable as organisms. Beyond this level, the units of the biosphere are those of the organism: organ systems composed of organs, organs of tissues, tissues of cells, cells of molecules, and molecules of atomic elements and energy. The progression, therefore, proceeding upward from atoms and energy, is toward fewer units, larger and more complex in pattern, at each successive level.

THE DIVERSITY OF LIFE

The biosphere supports between 3 and 30 million species of plants, animals, fungi, single-celled prokaryotes such as bacteria, and single-celled eukaryotes such as protozoans. Of this total, only about 1.4 million species have been named so far, and fewer than 1 percent have been studied for their ecological relationships and their role in ecosystems. A little more than half the named species are insects, which dominate terrestrial and freshwater communities worldwide; the laboratories of systematists are filled with insect species yet to be named and described. Hence, the relationships of organisms to their environments and the roles that species play in the biosphere are only beginning to be understood.

This tremendous diversity of life is organized into natural ecological groupings. As life has evolved, populations of organisms have become separated into different species that are reproductively isolated from one another. These species are organized through their interrelationships into complex biological communities. The interactions in

4

these communities affect, and are affected by, the physical environments in which they occur, thereby forming ecosystems through which the energy and nutrients necessary for life flow and cycle. The mix of species and physical environments vary across the globe, creating ecological communities, or biomes, such as the boreal forests of North America and Eurasia and the rainforests of the tropics. The sum total of the richness of these biomes is the biosphere.

This hierarchical organization of life has come about through the major processes of evolution—natural selection

One estimate of the number of known living species. The majority of species are still unknown—i.e., yet to be described by taxonomists. Encyclopædia Britannica, Inc.

(the differential success of the reproduction of hereditary variations resulting from the interaction of organisms with their environment), gene flow (the movement of genes among different populations of a species), and random genetic drift (the genetic change that occurs in small populations owing to chance). Natural selection operates on the expressed characteristics of genetic variants found within populations, winnowing members of the population who are less well suited to their environment from those better suited to it. In this manner, populations become adapted to their local ecosystems, which include both the physical environment and the other species with which they interact in order to survive and reproduce.

The genetic variation that is necessary for a species to adapt to the physical environment and to other organisms arises from new mutations within populations, the recombination of genes during sexual reproduction, and the migration of and interbreeding with individuals from other populations. In very small populations, however, some of that variation is lost by chance alone through random genetic drift. The combined result of these evolutionary processes is that after many generations populations of the same species have widely divergent characteristics. Some of these populations eventually become so genetically different that their members cannot successfully interbreed, resulting in the evolution of a separate species (that is, speciation).

The diversification of life through local adaptation of populations and speciation has created the tremendous biodiversity found on the Earth. In most regions a square kilometre (0.4 square mile) will harbour hundreds—in some places even thousands—of species. The interactions between these species create intricate webs of relationships as the organisms reciprocally evolve, adapting to one another and becoming specialized for their interactions. Natural communities of species reflect the sum of these species' interactions and the ongoing complex selection pressures they constantly endure that drive their evolution. The many ecological and evolutionary processes that affect the relationships among species and their environments render ecology one of the most intricate of the sciences. The answers to the major questions in ecology require an understanding of the relative effects of many variables acting simultaneously.

THE IMPORTANCE OF THE BIOSPHERE

The continued functioning of the biosphere is dependent not only on the maintenance of the intimate interactions among the myriad species within local communities but also on the looser yet crucial interactions of all species and communities around the globe. The Earth is blanketed with so many species and so many different kinds of biological communities because populations have been able to adapt to almost any kind of environment on Earth through natural selection. Life-forms have evolved that are able to survive in the ocean depths, the frigid conditions of Antarctica, and the near-boiling temperatures of geysers. The great richness of adaptations found among different populations and species of living organisms is the Earth's greatest resource. It is a richness that has evolved over millions of years and is irreplaceable.

It is therefore startling to realize that our inventory of the Earth's diversity is still so incomplete that the total number of living species cannot be estimated more closely than between 3 and 30 million species. Decades of continuous research must be carried out by systematists, ecologists, and geneticists before the inventory of biodiversity provides a more accurate count. The research has been slow. Only recently, as the extinction rate of species has been increasing rapidly, have societies begun to realize the interdependence of species. To sustain life on Earth, more than the few animal and plant species used by humans must be preserved. The flow of energy and the cycling of nutrients through ecosystems, the regulation of populations, and the stability of biological communities, all of which support the continued maintenance of life, rely on the diversity of species, their adaptations to local physical conditions, and their coevolved relationships.

Despite the limited scientific knowledge of most species, ecological studies during the 20th century have made great headway in unraveling the mechanisms by which organisms coevolve with one another and adapt to their physical environment, thereby shaping the biosphere. Each new decade has produced a steady stream of studies showing that the biological and physical elements of the Earth are more interconnected than had been previously thought. Those studies also have shown that often the most seemingly insignificant species are crucial to the stability of communities and ecosystems. Many seemingly obscure species are at risk worldwide of being dismissed as unimportant. The effect that the loss of species will have on ecosystems is appreciated only by understanding the relationships between organisms and their environments and by studying the ecological and evolutionary processes operating within ecosystems.

The need to understand how the biosphere functions has never been greater. When human population levels were low and technological abilities crude, societies' impact on the biosphere was relatively small. The increase in human population levels and the harvesting of more of the Earth's natural resources has altered this situation, especially in recent decades. Human activities are causing major alterations to the patterns of energy flow and nutrient cycling through ecosystems, and these activities are eliminating populations and species that have not even been described but which might have been of central importance to the maintenance of ecosystems.

The biologist Edward O. Wilson, who coined the term "biodiversity," estimated conservatively that in the late 20th century at least 27,000 species are becoming extinct each year. The majority of these are small tropical organisms. The impact that this freshet of extinctions would have on the biosphere is akin to receiving a box of engine parts and discarding a portion of them before reading the directions, assuming that their absence will have no negative repercussions on the running of the engine. The following sections describe how many of the biological and physical parts fit together to make the engine of the biosphere run and why many seemingly obscure species are important to the long-term functioning of the biosphere.

THE FLOW OF ENERGY

Most solar energy occurs at wavelengths unsuitable for photosynthesis. Between 98 and 99 percent of solar energy reaching the Earth is reflected from leaves and other surfaces and absorbed by other molecules, which convert it to heat. Thus, only 1 to 2 percent is available to be captured by plants. The rate at which plants photosynthesize depends on the amount of light reaching the leaves, the temperature of the environment, and the availability of water and other nutrients such as nitrogen and phosphorus. The measurement of the rate at which organisms

AVERAGE NET PRIMARY PRODUCTION OF THE EARTH'S MAJOR HABITATS	
HABITAT	NET PRIMARY PRODUCTION (GRAM PER SQUARE METRE PER YEAR)
Forests	
Tropical	1,800
Temperate	1,250
Boreal	800
Other terrestrial habitats	
Swamp and marsh	2,500
Savanna	700
Cultivated land	650
Shrubland	600
Desert scrub	70
Temperate grassland	500
Tundra and alpine	140
Aquatic habitats	
Algal beds and reefs	2,000
Estuaries	1,800
Lakes and streams	500
Continental shelf	360
Open ocean	125
Source: Adapted from Robert E. Ricklefs, *Ecology,* 3rd edition (1990), by W.H. Freeman and Company, used with permission.	

convert light energy (or inorganic chemical energy) to the chemical energy of organic compounds is called primary productivity. Hence, the total amount of energy assimilated by plants in an ecosystem during photosynthesis (gross primary productivity) varies among environments. (Productivity is often measured by an increase in biomass, a term used to refer to the weight of all living organisms in an area. Biomass is reported in grams or metric tons.)

Much of the energy assimilated by plants through photosynthesis is not stored as organic material but instead is used during cellular respiration. In this process organic compounds such as carbohydrates, proteins, and fats are broken down, or oxidized, to provide energy (in the form of adenosine triphosphate [ATP]) for the cell's metabolic needs. The energy not used in this process is stored in plant tissues for further use and is called net primary productivity. About 40 to 85 percent of gross primary productivity is not used during respiration and becomes net primary productivity. The highest net primary productivity in terrestrial environments occurs in swamps and marshes and tropical rainforests; the lowest occurs in deserts. In aquatic environments, the highest net productivity occurs in estuaries, algal beds, and reefs. Consequently, these environments are especially critical for the maintenance of worldwide biological productivity.

A small amount of the energy stored in plants, between 5 and 25 percent, passes into herbivores (plant eaters) as they feed, and a similarly small percentage of the energy in herbivores then passes into carnivores (animal eaters). The result is a pyramid of energy, with most energy concentrated in the photosynthetic organisms at the bottom of food chains and less energy at each higher trophic level (a division based on the main nutritional source of the organism). Some of the remaining energy does not pass directly into the plant-herbivore-carnivore food chain but instead is diverted into the detritus food chain. Bacteria, fungi, scavengers, and carrion eaters that consume detritus (detritivores) are all eventually consumed by other organisms.

The rate at which these consumers convert the chemical energy of their food into their own biomass is called secondary productivity. The efficiency at which energy is transferred from one trophic level to another is called ecological efficiency. On average it is estimated that there is only a 10 percent transfer of energy.

Energy is lost in several ways as it flows along these pathways of consumption. Most plant tissue is uneaten by herbivores, and this stored energy is therefore lost to the plant-herbivore-carnivore food chain. In terrestrial communities less than 10 percent of plant tissue is actually consumed by herbivores. The rest falls into the detritus pathway, although the detritivores consume only some of this decaying tissue. Oil and coal deposits are major repositories of this unused plant energy and have accumulated over long periods of geologic time.

The efficiency by which animals convert the food they ingest into energy for growth and reproduction is called assimilation efficiency. Herbivores assimilate between 15 and 80 percent of the plant material they ingest, depending on their physiology and the part of the plant that they eat. For example, herbivores that eat seeds and young vegetation high in energy have the highest assimilation efficiencies, those that eat older leaves have intermediate efficiencies, and those that feed on decaying wood have very low efficiencies. Carnivores generally have higher assimilation efficiencies than herbivores, often between 60 and 90 percent, because their food is more easily digested.

The overall productivity of the biosphere is therefore limited by the rate at which plants convert solar energy (about 1 percent) into chemical energy and the subsequent efficiencies at which other organisms at higher trophic levels convert that stored energy into their own biomass (approximately 10 percent). Human-induced changes in net primary productivity in the parts of the biosphere that have the highest productivity, such as estuaries and tropical moist forests, are likely to have large effects on the overall biological productivity of the Earth.

NUTRIENT CYCLING

The cells of all organisms are made up primarily of six major elements that occur in similar proportions in all life-forms. These elements—hydrogen, oxygen, carbon, nitrogen, phosphorus, and sulfur—form the core protoplasm of organisms, and the first four of these elements make up about 99 percent of the mass of most cells. Additional elements, however, are also essential to the growth of organisms. Calcium and other elements help to form cellular support structures such as shells, internal or external skeletons, and cell walls. Chlorophyll molecules, which allow photosynthetic plants to convert solar energy into chemical energy, are chains of carbon, hydrogen, and oxygen compounds built around a magnesium ion. Altogether, 16 elements are found in all organisms; another eight elements are found in some organisms but not in others.

These bioelements combine with one another to form a wide variety of chemical compounds. They occur in organisms in higher proportions than they do in the environment because organisms capture them, concentrating and combining them in various ways in their cells, and release them during metabolism and death. As a result, these essential nutrients alternate between inorganic and organic states as they rotate through their respective biogeochemical cycles. These cycles can include all or part of the following: the atmosphere, which is made up largely of gases including water vapour; the lithosphere, which encompasses the soil and the entire solid crust of the Earth; and the hydrosphere, which includes lakes, rivers, and oceans.

A portion of the elements are bound up in limestone and in the minerals of other rocks and are unavailable to organisms. The slow processes of weathering and erosion eventually release these elements to enter the cycle. For most of the major nutrients, however, organisms not only intercept the elements moving through the biosphere, but they actually drive the biogeochemical cycles.

The movement of nutrients through the biosphere is different from the transfer of energy because, whereas energy flows through the biosphere and cannot be reused, elements are recycled. The same molecule of carbon or nitrogen may, over the course of eons, move repeatedly between organisms, the atmosphere, the soil, and the oceans. A molecule of carbon released as carbon dioxide by an animal may remain in the atmosphere for 5 or 10 years before being taken up by another organism, or it may cycle almost immediately back into a neighbouring plant and be used during photosynthesis.

THE CARBON CYCLE

Life is built on the conversion of carbon dioxide into the carbon-based organic compounds of living organisms. The carbon cycle illustrates the central importance of carbon in the biosphere. Different paths of the carbon cycle recycle the element at varying rates. The slowest part of

AUTOTROPHS AND HETEROTROPHS

All life-forms can be categorized as either autotrophs or heterotrophs. Both groups play essential roles in food chains and nutrient cycling. An autotroph is an organism that serves as a primary producer in a food chain, whereas heterotrophs are organisms that consume other organisms.

Autotrophs obtain energy and nutrients by harnessing sunlight through photosynthesis (photoautotrophs) or, more rarely, obtain chemical energy through oxidation (chemoautotrophs) to make organic substances from inorganic ones. Autotrophs do not consume other organisms; they are, however, consumed by heterotrophs.

In contrast, heterotrophs are unable to produce organic substances from inorganic ones. They must rely on an organic source of carbon that has originated as part of another living organism. Heterotrophs depend either directly or indirectly on autotrophs for nutrients and food energy.

the cycle involves carbon that resides in sedimentary rocks, where most of the Earth's carbon is stored. When in contact with water that is acidic (pH is low), carbon will dissolve from bedrock; under neutral conditions, carbon will precipitate out as sediment such as calcium carbonate (limestone). This cycling between solution and precipitation is the background against which more rapid parts of the cycle occur.

Short-term cycling of carbon occurs in the continual physical exchange of carbon dioxide (CO_2) between the atmosphere and hydrosphere. Carbon dioxide from the atmosphere becomes dissolved in water (H_2O), with which it reacts to form carbonic acid (H_2CO_3), which dissociates into hydrogen ions (H^+) and bicarbonate ions (HCO_3^-), which further dissociate into hydrogen and carbonate ions (CO_3^{2-}). The more alkaline the water (pH above 7.0 is alkaline), the more carbon is present in the form of carbonate, as is shown in the following reversible reactions:

$$CO_2 + H_2O \rightleftharpoons H_2CO_3 \rightleftharpoons$$
$$H^+ + HCO_3^- \rightleftharpoons 2H^+ + CO_3^{2-}.$$

At the same time, carbon dioxide in the water is continually lost to the atmosphere. The exchange of carbon between the atmosphere and hydrosphere links the remaining parts of the cycle, which are the exchanges that occur between the atmosphere and terrestrial organisms and between water and aquatic organisms.

The biological cycling of carbon begins as photosynthetic organisms assimilate carbon dioxide or carbonates from the surrounding environment. In terrestrial communities, plants convert atmospheric carbon dioxide to carbon-based compounds through photosynthesis. During this process, plants cleave the carbon from the two oxygen molecules and release the oxygen back into the surrounding environment. Plants are thus primarily responsible for the presence of atmospheric oxygen. In aquatic communities, plants use dissolved carbon in the form of carbonates or carbon dioxide as the source of carbon for photosynthesis. Once carbon has been assimilated by photosynthetic organisms, as well as by the animals that eat them, it is released again in the form of carbon dioxide as these organisms respire. The release of carbon dioxide into the atmosphere or hydrosphere completes the biological part of the carbon cycle.

The pathways of the global carbon cycle, however, are never completely balanced. That is to say, carbon does not move in and out of all parts of the biosphere at equal rates. Consequently, over time some parts of the biosphere accumulate more carbon than others, thereby serving as major accessible carbon reservoirs. In preindustrial times the major reservoirs of carbon were the deep and shallow portions of the ocean; the soil, detritus, and biota of the land; and the atmosphere. The oceans were, and still are, the greatest reservoirs of carbon. Because marine phytoplankton have such short life cycles, the carbon in the ocean cycles rapidly between inorganic and organic states.

In terrestrial environments, forests are the largest carbon reservoirs. Up to 80 percent of the aboveground carbon in terrestrial communities and about a third of belowground carbon are contained within forests. Unlike the oceans, much of this carbon is stored directly in the tissues of plants. High-latitude forests include large amounts of carbon not only in aboveground vegetation but also in peat deposits. Forests at high and low latitudes particularly are important reservoirs of carbon. An estimated one-half of the carbon in forests occurs in high-latitude forests, and a little more than one-third occurs in low-latitude forests. The two largest forest reservoirs of carbon are the vast expanses in Russia, which hold roughly 25 percent of the world's forest carbon, and the Amazon basin, which contains about 20 percent.

Until recent centuries, the equilibrium between the carbon in the world's forests and in the atmosphere remained constant. Samples of carbon dioxide trapped in ice during the past 1,000 years and direct measurements of carbon dioxide in the atmosphere had remained fairly constant until the 18th century. However, the cutting of much of the world's forest is, along with the increase in consumption of fossil fuels attendant on the Industrial Revolution, has resulted in a disruption of the balance between the amount of carbon dioxide in the forests and in the atmosphere. The concentration of atmospheric carbon dioxide has been increasing steadily; currently the rate of increase is about 4 percent per decade. If human activities continue to alter the relative sizes of the carbon reservoirs worldwide, they are likely to have large effects on the carbon cycle and other biogeochemical cycles. Large-scale deforestation in Russia and the Amazon basin are likely to have particularly significant effects on global carbon storage and cycling.

The warming of global temperatures also is changing which ecosystems act as long-term sinks for carbon and which act as sources for carbon dioxide in the atmosphere. For example, the Arctic tundra, with large amounts of carbon stored in its soils, has been a net sink for carbon dioxide during long periods of geologic time. The recent warming of many Arctic regions, however, has accelerated the rate of soil decomposition, transforming these Arctic areas into potential sources of atmospheric carbon dioxide.

The complex cycle of carbon and the varying sizes of carbon reservoirs illustrate some of the reasons it has been so difficult to predict the effects that increased atmospheric carbon will have on global change.

THE NITROGEN CYCLE

Nitrogen is one of the elements most likely to be limiting to plant growth. Like carbon, nitrogen has its own biogeochemical cycle, circulating through the atmosphere, lithosphere, and hydrosphere. Unlike carbon, which is stored primarily in sedimentary rock, most nitrogen occurs in the atmosphere as an inorganic compound (N_2). It is the predominant atmospheric gas, making up about 79 percent of the volume of the atmosphere. Plants, however, cannot use nitrogen in its gaseous form and are able to assimilate it only after it has been converted to ammonia (NH_3) and nitrates (NO_3^-). This reductive process, called nitrogen fixation, is a chemical reaction in which electrons are picked up from another molecule. A small amount of nitrogen is fixed by lightning, but most of the nitrogen harvested from the atmosphere is removed by nitrogen-fixing bacteria and cyanobacteria (formerly called blue-green algae).

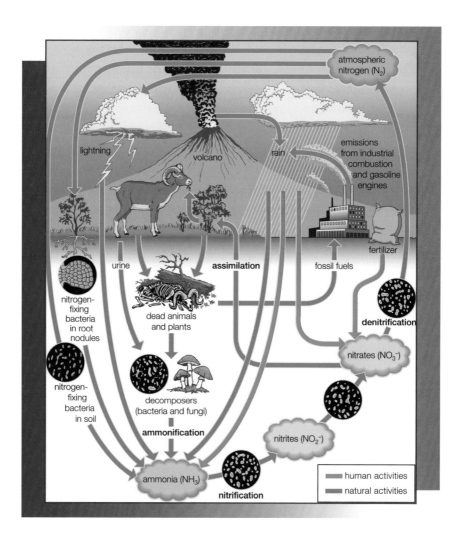

The nitrogen cycle. Encyclopædia Britannica, Inc.

Certain species of nitrogen-fixing bacteria can coexist intimately (symbiotically) with legumes and other plants, providing the plants with necessary nitrogen. In this symbiotic association, the bacteria become encased in nodules that grow on the roots of plants, through which nitrogen that has been fixed by the resident bacteria is obtained. Cyanobacteria have developed similar relationships with various life-forms, such as liverworts, hornworts, cycads, and at least one genus of flowering plants (*Gunnera*). Their symbiotic relationship with fungi has earned its own designation—the coexistent species are called lichen.

Other microorganisms perform important tasks that propel the nitrogen cycle along. Although plants can assimilate ammonia as well as nitrates, most of the ammonia in the soil is converted to nitrites (NO_2^-) and then to nitrates by certain aerobic bacteria through the oxidative process of nitrification. Once nitrogen has been assimilated by plants, it can be converted to organic forms, such as amino acids and proteins. Animals can use only organic nitrogen, which they obtain by consuming plants or other animals. As these organisms die, certain microbes such as detritivores are able to participate in the decomposition of organic nitrogen into ammonia (ammonification), providing a constant supply of ammonia to be used in the process of nitrification. Although the fixation of atmospheric nitrogen is an essential part of the nitrogen cycle, ammonification and nitrification are the predominant methods by which organic nitrogen is prevented from returning to the atmosphere and is kept cycling through the biosphere.

Some nitrogen does return to the atmosphere, however, as denitrifying bacteria break down nitrates to obtain oxygen, thereby releasing gaseous N_2. Nitrogen is also lost from plants and soil in terrestrial environments via other routes, including erosion, runoff, volatilization of ammonia into the atmosphere, and leaching from soils into lakes and streams. Eventually some of these nutrients reach the oceans as rivers flush them onto the ocean surface.

THE SULFUR CYCLE

Sulfur is found in all living organisms as a constituent of some proteins, vitamins, and hormones. Like carbon and nitrogen, sulfur cycles between the atmosphere, lithosphere, and hydrosphere; but, unlike these two other elements, it has major reservoirs in both the atmosphere and the lithosphere. As is true in the nitrogen cycle, the activities of microorganisms are crucial in the global cycling of this nutrient.

The process begins with geochemical and meteorologic processes such as the weathering of rock. When sulfur is released from the rock and comes in contact with air, it is converted into sulfate (SO_4), which is taken up by plants and microorganisms and converted into organic forms. Animals acquire these organic forms of sulfur from their foods. When organisms die and decompose, some of the sulfur enters the tissues of microorganisms and some is released again as sulfate. There is, however, a continual loss of sulfur from terrestrial ecosystems as some of it drains into lakes and streams and eventually into the ocean as runoff. Additional sulfur enters the ocean through fallout from the atmosphere.

Once in the ocean, some of the sulfur cycles through marine communities as it moves through food chains, some reenters the atmosphere, and some is lost to the ocean depths as it combines with iron to form ferrous sulfide (FeS), which is responsible for the black colour of marine sediments. Sulfur reenters the atmosphere naturally in three major ways: sea spray releases large amounts of the element from the ocean into the atmosphere; anaerobic respiration by sulfate-reducing bacteria causes the release of hydrogen sulfide (H_2S) gas especially from marshes, tidal flats, and similar environments in which anaerobic microorganisms thrive; and volcanic activity releases additional but much smaller amounts of sulfur gas into the atmosphere.

Since the Industrial Revolution, human activities have contributed significantly to the movement of sulfur from the lithosphere to the atmosphere as the burning of fossil fuels and the processing of metals have occasioned large emissions of sulfur dioxide. Oxides of sulfur and nitrogen contribute to the acid rain that is common downwind from these industrial activities.

THE PHOSPHORUS CYCLE

Most other major nutrients such as phosphorus, potassium, magnesium, iron, and calcium enter terrestrial communities through the weathering of bedrock. These nutrients lack a volatile gaseous state. Consequently, they cycle through the biosphere differently from carbon, nitrogen, and sulfur, all of which sometimes occur as volatile gases. Of the nonvolatile nutrients, phosphorus is the one that most often limits plant growth, especially in aquatic environments.

Phosphorus and the other nonvolatile elements move unidirectionally from land, through aquatic environments, into ocean sediments. Most phosphorus cycling occurs between the surface and depths of the ocean. When near the surface, phosphorus is taken up by the plankton and passed through the food chain. It cycles back to the ocean bottom as individuals die and fall to the ocean floor, releasing assimilated phosphorus. Much of this element gradually accumulates in the ocean sediment as particulate phosphorus and is eventually brought back to the surface only through ocean upwelling and tectonic activity. The ocean sediments are therefore by far the greatest reservoirs of phosphorus.

In terrestrial ecosystems, much of the available phosphorus moves in a closed cycle between living organisms and the organic debris in the soil. Phosphate (PO_4^{3-}) is the only important inorganic form involved in this cycle. Microorganisms in the soil break down litter and other organic matter, thereby releasing phosphate, which is then taken up by plants and released again when they die and decompose. Soils differ in the amount of phosphorus they contain, and in some phosphorus-poor soils almost all the available phosphorus resides in living organisms and organic debris. In some tropical forests, such as those in parts of Brazil, so much of the phosphorus is contained in living organisms that the clearing of forests eliminates most of this element. As a result, the plant communities cannot recover, and crops cannot be grown.

The addition of phosphorus to soils poor in this nutrient and the use of phosphorus-rich detergents have had a great impact on the phosphorus cycle in many ecosystems. Runoff from agricultural fields and the emptying of sewage has introduced so much extra phosphorus to rivers and lakes that populations of plants and microorganisms have grown explosively, sometimes creating a solid mat that extends over the surface of the water. This growth increases the amount of organic debris in the water, which can lead to a decrease in the available oxygen, resulting in suffocation of fish and other animals.

THE HYDROLOGIC CYCLE

A portion of the biogeochemical cycle of all elements involves time spent cycling through the hydrosphere.

Water itself cycles within the biosphere. Unlike the cycles of the other major nutrients, however, the hydrologic, or water, cycle would continue in some form even in the absence of living organisms. Most of the Earth's water is in its core, in the sedimentary rocks near its surface, and in the ocean. A minute percentage of the water, however, continually cycles through the atmosphere, oceans, and terrestrial environments mainly by the processes of evaporation and precipitation.

This part of the hydrologic cycle is driven by solar energy. Water evaporates from both the aquatic and terrestrial environments as it is heated by the Sun's energy. The rates of evaporation and precipitation depend on solar energy, as do the patterns of circulation of moisture in the air and currents in the ocean. Evaporation exceeds precipitation over the oceans, and this water vapour is transported by the wind over land, where it returns to the land through precipitation. The water falling onto terrestrial environments seeps into the ground or runs off into lakes and streams and eventually empties into the oceans, carrying with it many of the other major nutrients. Water also reenters the atmosphere through the evaporative loss of water by plants (transpiration).

LINKS AMONG THE NUTRIENT CYCLES

Although the overall pattern of cycling of all the major elements is now known, there is still much to learn about the relative importance of the different stages of each cycle. For example, there is considerable debate concerning which ecosystems act as the major sources of carbon for the atmosphere and which act as sinks by accumulating more carbon than they release. The ways in which the different cycles interact with one another also must be minutely studied. It has been discovered that sulfur availability influences the rate of nitrogen accumulation in plants and nitrogen availability influences phosphorus uptake. All three elements are thought to influence the rate of carbon accumulation by plants. As a result, changes in any one of these nutrient cycles influence the other cycles as well.

The effects that disruptions in these cycles may have within the biosphere are not clearly understood. Natural geologic phenomena, such as ice ages and major periods of volcanic activity, have repeatedly disturbed these cycles throughout Earth history. Many human activities may have impacts of similar scope. Deforestation, the burning of fossil fuels, and increased fertilization are disturbing these cycles. These anthropogenic disturbances have increased atmospheric levels of carbon dioxide, decreased ozone (O_3) levels, and undermined the natural equilibrium of streams and lakes by excessive nutrient enrichment from sewage, fertilizers, and factory waste (cultural eutrophication). Gleaning more information about the biogeochemical cycles and their interactions has become increasingly important now that the effects of human activities are becoming more apparent.

Another potential effect that may result from human intrusions in the environment is global warming. Carbon dioxide in the atmosphere has the ability to act as an insulator, preventing some of the Earth's heat, absorbed from solar radiation, from escaping back into space. This process, known as the greenhouse effect, is suspected of being enhanced by rising levels of atmospheric carbon dioxide, which have resulted in part from the combustion of fossil fuels and the clearing and burning of tropical forests. This increase in atmospheric carbon dioxide and other so-called greenhouse gases could raise the overall global temperature, causing the polar ice caps to melt, sea levels to rise, and the Earth's precipitation to be redistributed.

The complexity and interconnectedness of each of the biogeochemical cycles make it difficult to pinpoint how any one human activity is altering the cycles; nevertheless, the majority of those who study these fluctuations agree that this is happening. Disagreements generally concern the extent to which various activities affect particular cycles and what the long-term consequences of these disturbances will be.

EARTH'S ENVIRONMENTAL CONDITIONS

Most organisms are limited to either a terrestrial or an aquatic environment. An organism's ability to tolerate local conditions within its environment further restricts its distribution. One parameter, such as temperature tolerance, may be important in determining the limits of distribution, but often a combination of variables, such as temperature tolerance and water requirements, is important. Extreme environmental variables can evoke physiological and behavioral responses from organisms. The physiological response helps the organism maintain a constant internal environment (homeostasis), while a behavioral response allows it to avoid the environmental challenge—a fallback strategy if homeostasis cannot be maintained.

The ways in which modern living organisms tolerate environmental conditions reflect the aquatic origins of life. With few exceptions, life cannot exist outside the temperature range at which water is a liquid. Thus, liquid water, and temperatures that maintain water as a liquid, are essential for sustaining life. Within those parameters, the concentrations of dissolved salts and other ions, the abundance of respiratory gases, atmospheric or hydrostatic pressure, and rate of water flow all influence the physiology, behaviour, and distribution of organisms.

THE ROLE OF TEMPERATURE

Temperature has the single most important influence on the distribution of organisms because it determines the physical state of water. Most organisms cannot live in conditions in which the temperature remains below 0 °C (32 °F) or above 45 °C (113 °F) for any length of time. Adaptations have enabled certain species to survive outside this range—thermophilic bacteria have been found in hot springs in which the temperatures may approach the boiling point, and certain polar mosses and lichens can tolerate temperatures of -70 °C (–94 °F), but these species are the exceptions. Few organisms can remain for long periods at temperatures above 45 °C, because organic molecules such as proteins will begin to denature. Nor are temperatures below freezing conducive to life: cells will rupture if the water they contain freezes.

Most organisms are not able to maintain a body temperature that is significantly different from that of the environment. Sessile organisms, such as plants and fungi, and very small organisms and animals that cannot move great distances, therefore, must be able to withstand the full range of temperatures sustained by their habitat. In contrast, many mobile animals employ behavioral mechanisms to avoid extreme conditions in the short term. Such behaviours vary from simply moving short distances out of the Sun or an icy wind to large-scale migrations.

Some types of animals employ physiological mechanisms to maintain a constant body temperature, and two categories are commonly distinguished: the term "cold-blooded" is understood to refer to reptiles and invertebrates, and "warm-blooded" is generally applied to mammals and birds. These terms, however, are imprecise; the more accurate terms, ectotherm for cold-blooded and endotherm for warm-blooded, are more useful in describing the thermal capabilities of these animals. Ectotherms rely on external sources of heat to regulate their body temperatures, and endotherms thermoregulate by generating heat internally.

Terrestrial ectotherms utilize the complex temperature profile of the terrestrial environment to derive warmth. They can absorb solar radiation, thus raising their body temperatures above that of the surrounding air and substrate, unlike the aquatic ectotherm, whose body

Cold-blooded creatures such as lizards regulate their body temperature by basking in the sun, soaking up solar radiation and heat. DEA/Baldizzone/ De Agostini Picture Library/Getty Images

temperature is usually very close to that of the environment. As this solar radiation is taken up, physiological mechanisms contribute to the regulation of heat—peripheral blood vessels dilate and heart rate increases. The animal also may employ behavioral mechanisms, such as reorienting itself toward the Sun or flattening its body and spreading its legs to maximize its surface area exposure. At night, loss of heat may be reduced by other behavioral and physiological mechanisms—the heart rate may slow, peripheral blood vessels may constrict, surface area may be minimized, and shelter may be sought.

Endotherms maintain body temperature independently of the environment by the metabolic production of heat. They generate heat internally and control passive heat loss by varying the quality of their insulation or by repositioning themselves to alter their effective surface area (i.e., curling into a tight ball). If heat loss exceeds heat generation, metabolism increases to make up the loss. If heat generation exceeds the rate of loss, mechanisms to increase heat loss by evaporation occur. In either case, behavioral mechanisms can be employed to seek a more suitable thermal environment.

To survive for a limited period in adverse conditions, endotherms may employ a combination of behavioral and physiological mechanisms. In cold weather, which requires an increase in energy consumption, the animal may enter a state of torpor in which its body temperature, metabolism, respiratory rate, and heart rate are depressed. Long-term winter hypothermia, or hibernation, is an extended state of torpor that some animals use as a response to cold conditions. Torpor and hibernation free the animals from energetically expensive maintenance of high body temperatures, saving energy when food is limited.

Another form of torpor, estivation, is experienced by animals in response to heat stress. This state is seen more often in ectothermic animals than in endotherms, but in both the stimulus for estivation is usually a combination of high temperatures and water shortage.

Humidity

Most terrestrial organisms must maintain their water content within fairly narrow limits. Water commonly is lost to the air through evaporation or, in plants, transpiration. Because most water loss occurs by diffusion and the rate of diffusion is determined by the gradient across the diffusion barrier such as the surface of a leaf or skin, the rate of water loss will depend on the relative humidity of the air. Relative humidity is the percent saturation of air relative to its total saturation possible at a given temperature. When air is totally saturated, relative humidity is said to be 100 percent. Cool air that is completely saturated contains less water vapour than completely saturated warm air because the water vapour capacity of warm air is greater. Diffusion gradients across skin or leaves, therefore, can be much steeper in summer when the air is warm, rendering evaporative water loss a much more serious problem in warm environments than in cool environments. Nevertheless, rates of water loss are higher in dry air (conditions of low relative humidity) than in moist air (conditions of high relative humidity), regardless of the temperature.

Water loss from evaporation must be compensated by water uptake from the environment. For most plants, transpirational water loss is countered by the uptake of water from the soil via roots. For animals, water content can be replenished by eating or drinking or by uptake through the integument. For organisms living in dry environments, there are many morphological and physiological mechanisms that reduce water loss. Desert plants, or xerophytes, typically have reduced leaf surface areas because leaves are the major sites of transpiration. Some xerophytes shed their leaves altogether in summer, and some are dormant during the dry season.

Desert animals typically have skin that is relatively impervious to water. The major site of evaporation is the respiratory exchange surface, which must be moist to allow the gaseous exchange of oxygen and carbon dioxide. A reduction in amount of water lost through respiration can occur if the temperature of the exhaled air is lower than the temperature of the body. As many animals, such as gazelles, inhale warm air, heat and water vapour from the nasal passages evaporate, cooling the nose and the blood within it. The cool venous blood passes close to and cools the warm arterial blood traveling to the brain. If the brain does not require cooling, the venous blood returns to the heart by another route. The nasal passages also cool the warm, saturated air from the lungs so that water condenses in the nose and is reabsorbed rather than lost to the environment.

THE pH SCALE

The relative acidity or alkalinity of a solution is reported by the pH scale, which is a measure of the concentration of hydrogen ions in solution. Neutral solutions have a pH of 7. A pH of less than 7 denotes acidity (an increased hydrogen ion concentration), and above 7 alkalinity (a decreased hydrogen ion concentration). Many important molecular processes within the cells of organisms occur within a very narrow range of pH. Thus, maintenance of internal pH by homeostatic mechanisms is vital for cells to function properly. Although pH may differ locally within an organism, most tissues are within one pH unit of neutral. Because aquatic organisms generally have somewhat permeable skins or respiratory exchange surfaces, external conditions can influence internal pH. These organisms may accomplish the extremely important task of regulating internal pH by exchanging hydrogen ions for other ions, such as sodium or bicarbonate, with the environment.

The pH of naturally occurring waters can range from very acidic conditions of about 3 in peat swamps to very alkaline conditions of about 9 in alkaline lakes. Naturally acidic water may result from the presence of organic acids, as is the case in a peat swamp, or from geologic conditions such as sulfur deposits associated with volcanic activity. Naturally occurring alkaline waters usually result from inorganic sources. Most organisms are unable to live in conditions of extreme alkalinity or acidity.

THE SALINITY OF EARTH'S WATER BODIES

The term "salinity" refers to the amount of dissolved salts that are present in water. Sodium and chloride are the predominant ions in seawater, and the concentrations of magnesium, calcium, and sulfate ions are also substantial. Naturally occurring waters vary in salinity from the almost pure water, devoid of salts, in snowmelt to the saturated solutions in salt lakes such as the Dead Sea. Salinity in the oceans is constant but is more variable along the coast where seawater is diluted with freshwater from runoff or from the emptying of rivers. This brackish water forms a barrier separating marine and freshwater organisms.

The cells of organisms also contain solutions of dissolved ions, but the range of salinity that occurs in tissues is more narrow than the range that occurs in nature.

Although a minimum number of ions must be present in the cytoplasm for the cell to function properly, excessive concentrations of ions will impair cellular functioning. Organisms that live in aquatic environments and whose integument is permeable to water, therefore, must be able to contend with osmotic pressure. This pressure arises if two solutions of unequal solute concentration exist on either side of a semipermeable membrane such as the skin. Water from the solution with a lower solute concentration will cross the membrane diluting the more highly concentrated solution until both concentrations are equalized. If the salt concentration of an animal's body fluids is higher than that of the surrounding environment, the osmotic pressure will cause water to diffuse through the skin until the concentrations are equal unless some mechanism prevents this from happening.

Many marine invertebrates have the same osmotic pressure as seawater. When the salt concentration of their surroundings changes, however, they must be able to adjust. Two means of contending with this situation are employed, and, depending on how they regulate the salt concentrations of their tissues, organisms are classified as osmoregulators or osmoconformers. The osmotic concentration of the body fluids of an osmoconformer changes to match that of its external environment, whereas an osmoregulator controls the osmotic concentration of its body fluids, keeping them constant in spite of external alterations. Aquatic organisms that can tolerate a wide range of external ion concentrations are called euryhaline; those that have a limited tolerance are called stenohaline.

Even if aquatic organisms have an integument that is relatively impermeable to water, as well as to small inorganic ions, their respiratory exchange surfaces are permeable. Hence, organisms occurring in water that has

Sharks have adapted to the salinity of sea water through a metabolic process that produces higher concentrations of salt in their tissues. This stems the buildup of sodium ions in their bodies. Franco Banfi/Photographer's Choice/Getty Images

a lower solute concentration than their tissues (e.g., trout in mountain streams) will constantly lose ions to the environment as water flows into their tissues. In contrast, organisms in salty environments face a constant loss of water and an influx of ions.

Many mechanisms have evolved that deal with these problems. Because water cannot be readily pumped across cell membranes, salinity balance is usually maintained by actively transporting inorganic ions, usually sodium and chloride. This process consumes energy and can usurp a large portion of the energy budget of animals in very saline environments. In marine fish, gill cells pump ions out of the body into the sea, while in freshwater fish gill cells pump ions in the opposite direction. Passive water loss in marine fish is compensated primarily in one of two ways. Most bony fish drink copiously and excrete salt across the gills, while the majority of sharks artificially elevate the salt concentration of their tissues above that of seawater with urea and other organic molecules, allowing water to slowly and passively enter the body. Through their food and across their gills, freshwater fish replenish most of the ions they lose. They also produce large quantities of very dilute urine to excrete excess water that diffuses into their bodies.

WATER CURRENTS

The flow of water presents special problems for aquatic organisms. Flow is associated with rivers, oceanic currents, and waves and can be laminar (streamlined) or turbulent. Many organisms are specialized to live in flowing environments; the main obstacle to this lifestyle is the constant threat of being washed away. Both plants and animals have evolved mechanisms that help to anchor them to the substratum in flowing water (e.g., the holdfast of kelp or the byssus threads of mussels). If anchorage can be assured, there are many advantages to living in this environment. Flowing water generally is well oxygenated, and the supply is continuous; nutrients and food are constantly replenished as well. The very precariousness of the environment also affords some protection from predation because the number of predators that make this type of habitat home is limited.

ATMOSPHERIC PRESSURE

Variations in atmospheric pressure can present special problems for the respiratory systems of animals because atmospheric pressure affects the exchange of oxygen and carbon dioxide that occurs during animal respiration. Normal atmospheric pressure at sea level is the total pressure that a column of air above the surface of the Earth exerts (760 mm of mercury, or 1 atmosphere). The total pressure is the sum of the pressures that each gas—mainly nitrogen, oxygen, and carbon dioxide—would exert alone (the partial pressure of that gas). As an animal breathes, oxygen moves from the environment across the respiratory surfaces into the blood; carbon dioxide moves in the reverse direction. This process occurs primarily by passive diffusion; each gas moves from an area of greater to lesser partial pressure, driven by the differential that exists across the respiratory surface. At higher altitudes, where the atmospheric pressure is lower, the partial pressure of oxygen is also lower. The partial pressure differential of oxygen, therefore, is also lower, and the organism effectively receives less oxygen when it breathes, even though the percentage of oxygen in the air remains constant. This lack of oxygen is why humans carry oxygen when ascending to high altitudes. Humans who live in mountainous regions, however, can become acclimatized to the lowered availability of oxygen, and certain animals such as llamas have adaptations of the blood that allow them to live at high altitudes. Birds have very efficient lungs, and many apparently have no problems flying to high altitudes, even for extended flights.

HYDROSTATIC PRESSURE

Because air and water have vastly different densities, the pressures experienced in terrestrial and aquatic habitats differ markedly. A column of water, so much denser than air, exerts a greater amount of pressure than a column of air. With each 10-metre (32.8-foot) increase in depth, there is an increase in hydrostatic pressure equivalent to one atmosphere. Mean ocean depth is about 3,800 metres (about 12,500 feet) and has a pressure of about 380 atmospheres. To surmount this environmental challenge, animals that live at great depths lack air compartments such as lungs or swim bladders. Surface-dwelling animals that dive to great depths meet this challenge differently. As pressure increases during a dive, air compartments compress, returning to their former volume when the animal surfaces. Air is forced into the trachea, bronchi, and bronchioles, where no gas uptake occurs. Thus, the increased pressure cannot drive more gases into the bloodstream, and, as the animal rises, it does not experience the "bends" (decompression sickness resulting from a rapid reduction of air pressure). In contrast, sea snakes avoid the bends by excreting nitrogen across the skin to offset the uptake of this gas from the lungs.

CHAPTER 2
THE EVOLUTION OF THE BIOSPHERE

Life is characteristic of the Earth. The biosphere—which in relation to the diameter of the Earth is an extremely thin, life-supporting layer between the upper troposphere and the superficial layers of porous rocks and sediments—is clearly visible from space; it is responsible for the blue and green colours seen in satellite photographs of the Earth.

All known forms of life are based on nucleic acid–protein systems, although life systems involving different chemical components are theoretically possible. Life appears to have developed on Earth as soon as conditions permitted. Cooling of the hot, primordial Earth was an important factor. In a universe in which extremes of temperature are the norm, most life-forms are restricted to a relatively narrow range of about 0 to 100 °C (32 to 212 °F).

The abiotic elements of the biosphere have been profoundly shaped by life, just as life has been molded by the environmental conditions that surround it. The biosphere has grown over time. Seven hundred million years ago it was a narrow and possibly discontinuous band encompassing only the shallower parts of the ocean. Today it reaches high into the atmosphere and deep into the ocean, invading even the tiny spaces in porous rocks. Thus, from the troposphere, which extends from 10 to 17 km (6.2 to 9.9 miles) above sea level, to the deepest parts of the ocean (11 km [about 7 miles] below the sea), to many hundreds of metres into the rocks of the Earth's crust, life thrives.

Even in the most hostile of the Earth's environments—the frozen and parched south polar desert—algae find refuge in tiny spaces in translucent rocks. The rocks provide shelter from the wind and focus the rays of the Sun, acting as a greenhouse and allowing biological activity to take place for a few weeks each year. At the other extreme, there are thermophilic (heat-loving) bacteria inhabiting deep-sea volcanic vents in which the water is heated under immense pressure to extremely high temperatures. Some researchers believe that some hyperthermophilic organisms existing in these vents can survive at temperatures above 300 °C (572 °F). If the temperature drops much below the boiling point, they die.

Life is changed through the process of evolution. Evolution is an inevitable consequence of inheritance, genetic variation, and competition arising from the number of individuals exceeding available resources. The result—natural selection—permits the perpetuation of some traits over others. Through billions of years this process has resulted in a great diversification of life-forms.

The history of life is characterized by an acceleration of evolutionary change and unpredictable periods of extinction, often followed by rapid diversification. There is still much debate over the causes—and even the importance—of some of these trends and events. Perhaps the most hotly debated issues at present concern theories of extinction and diversification. In the early 1970s the evolutionary biologists Stephen Jay Gould and Niles Eldredge developed a model called "punctuated equilibrium," which describes and explains some aspects of speciation. This theory postulates that evolution does not progress at a steady rate but rather in bursts, as brief periods of rapid evolutionary change are followed by long periods of relative evolutionary stasis.

The degree of interdependence between organic and inorganic elements of the biosphere and the importance of both negative and positive feedback mechanisms in the maintenance of life increasingly are being recognized. At one extreme the British physicist James Lovelock and the American microbiologist Lynn Margulis have argued that, because the elements of the biosphere are so interdependent and interrelated, the biosphere can be viewed as a single, self-regulating organism, which they call Gaia.

The Gaia hypothesis postulates that the physical conditions of the Earth's surface, oceans, and atmosphere have been made fit and comfortable for life and have been maintained in this state by the biota themselves. Evidence includes the relatively constant temperature of the Earth's surface that has been maintained for the past 3.5 billion years despite a 25 percent increase in energy coming from the Sun during that period. The remarkable constancy of the Earth's oceanic and atmospheric chemistry for the past 500 million years also is invoked to support this theory.

Also integral to the Gaia hypothesis is the crucial involvement of the biota in the cycling of various elements vital to life. The role that living things play in both the carbon and sulfur cycles is a good example of the importance of biological activity and the complex interrelationship of organic and inorganic elements in the biosphere.

Although the Gaia concept has provided intriguing models of the biosphere, many researchers do not believe the biosphere to be as fully integrated as the Gaia hypothesis suggests.

EARTH'S GEOLOGIC HISTORY AND EARLY LIFE-FORMS

The Earth is approximately 4.6 billion years old. The oldest minerals known are zircon crystals found in western Australia that are about 4.4 billion years old. The oldest known rocks were found in Greenland and are 4.28 billion years old. They formed at a time when the Earth

LYNN MARGULIS

(b. March 5, 1938, Chicago, Ill., U.S.)

Lynn Margulis is an American biologist whose serial endosymbiotic theory of eukaryotic cell development revolutionized the modern concept of how life arose on Earth.

Margulis was raised in Chicago. Intellectually precocious, she graduated with a bachelor's degree from the University of Chicago in 1957. Soon after, she married American astronomer Carl Sagan, with whom she had two children; one, Dorion, would become her frequent collaborator. The couple divorced in 1964. Margulis earned a master's degree in zoology and genetics from the University of Wisconsin at Madison in 1960 and a Ph.D. in genetics from the University of California, Berkeley, in 1965. She joined the biology department of Boston University in 1966 and taught there until 1988, when she was named distinguished university professor in the department of botany at the University of Massachusetts at Amherst. She retained that title when her affiliation at the university changed to the department of biology in 1993 and then to the department of geosciences in 1997.

Throughout most of her career, Margulis was considered a radical by peers who pursued traditional Darwinian "survival of the fittest" approaches to biology. Her ideas, which focused on symbiosis—a living arrangement of two different organisms in an association that can be either beneficial or unfavourable—were frequently greeted with skepticism and even hostility. Among her most important work was the development of the serial endosymbiotic theory (SET) of the origin of cells, which posits that eukaryotic cells (cells with nuclei) evolved from the symbiotic merger of nonnucleated bacteria that had previously existed independently. In this theory, mitochondria and chloroplasts, two major organelles of eukaryotic cells, are descendants of once free-living bacterial species. She explained the concept in her first book, *Origin of Eukaryotic Cells* (1970). At the time, her theory was regarded as far-fetched, but it has since been widely accepted. She elaborated in her 1981 classic, *Symbiosis in Cell Evolution*, proposing that another symbiotic merger of cells with bacteria—this time spirochetes, a type of bacterium that undulates rapidly—developed into the internal transportation system of the nucleated cell. Margulis further postulated that eukaryotic cilia were also originally spirochetes and that cytoplasm evolved from a symbiotic relationship between eubacteria and archaebacteria.

Her 1982 book *Five Kingdoms*, written with American biologist Karlene V. Schwartz, articulates a five-kingdom system of classifying life on Earth—animals, plants, bacteria (prokaryotes), fungi, and protoctists. The protist kingdom, which comprises most unicellular organisms (and multicellular algaes) in other systems, is rejected as too general. Many of the organisms usually categorized as protists are placed in one of the other four kingdoms; protoctists make up the remaining organisms, which are all aquatic, and include algaes and slime molds. Margulis edited portions of the compendium *Handbook of Protoctista* (1990).

Another area of interest for Margulis was her long collaboration with British scientist James Lovelock on the controversial Gaia hypothesis. This proposes that the Earth can be viewed as a single self-regulating organism—that is, a complex entity whose living and inorganic elements are interdependent and whose life-forms actively modify the environment to maintain hospitable conditions.

In addition to Margulis's scholarly publications, she wrote numerous books interpreting scientific concepts and quandaries for a popular audience. Among them were *Mystery Dance: On the Evolution of Human Sexuality* (1991), *What Is Life?* (1995), *What Is Sex?* (1997), and *Dazzle Gradually: Reflections on Nature in Nature* (2007), all cowritten with her son. She also wrote a book of stories, *Luminous Fish* (2007). Her later efforts were published under the Sciencewriters Books imprint of Chelsea Green Publishing, which she cofounded with Dorion in 2006.

Margulis was elected to the National Academy of Sciences in 1983 and was one of three American members of the Russian Academy of Natural Sciences. She was awarded the William Procter Prize of Sigma Xi, an international research society, and the U.S. National Medal of Science in 1999. In 2008 she received the Darwin-Wallace Medal of the Linnean Society of London.

was fiery with volcanic activity and pummeled by meteorites. During this time, sometimes referred to as the Hadean Eon, no atmosphere, ozone layer, continents, or oceans existed, and life could not be supported under such conditions.

The formation of the atmosphere is believed to have resulted from the release of gases from volcanic eruptions (one example of outgassing). As the surface of the Earth cooled, water vapour in the newly formed atmosphere condensed to form the water of the oceans. Until about 4 billion years ago the oceans may have been too hot to support life. By 2.8 billion years ago the first lightweight silica and aluminum rocks, which are typical of the continents, had formed. These rocks expanded rapidly so that by 2.6 billion years ago as much as 60 percent of the continental masses in existence today had formed, and the processes that permit continental drift had commenced.

THE DEVELOPMENT OF LIFE

The oldest undisputed fossils are about 3.5 billion years old. Life seems to have originated about 3.9 to 3.5 billion years ago. The basic chemical building blocks needed to form life are abundant on the Earth as well as elsewhere in the known universe. Life probably first arose through the self-assembly of small, organic molecules into larger ones. The surface of clays or crystals may have acted as a template in this process. Dehydration and freezing also may have played a role in the assembly of more complex molecules.

During a series of famous experiments in the 1950s by Stanley Miller and Harold C. Urey at the University of Chicago, atmospheric conditions predominating on Earth during the Archean Eon (3.8? to 2.5 billion years ago) were simulated. An electric spark, which substituted for lightning, was introduced to a mixture of gases that reacted to form amino acids, the basic building blocks of proteins. Later experiments produced the nucleotide bases that make up the structure of DNA. How these basic building blocks were assembled to form life remains unclear. The process may have taken many millions of years.

THE FIRST LIFE-FORMS

The earliest simple life-forms in the fossil record are prokaryotes (cellular organisms without a membrane-enclosed nucleus)—namely, the bacteria and cyanobacteria (formerly called blue-green algae). They have been found in rocks called stromatolites, structures that are layered, globular, generally calcareous, and often larger than a football. Stromatolites formed when colonies of prokaryotes became trapped in sediments; they are easily identifiable fossils, obvious to a researcher in the field. Thin-sectioning of fossil stromatolites occasionally reveals the microscopic, fossilized cells of the organisms that made them.

Until about 2.5 to 2.8 billion years ago, the Earth's atmosphere was largely composed of carbon dioxide. As primitive bacteria and cyanobacteria had, through photosynthesis or related life processes, captured atmospheric carbon, depositing it on the seafloor, carbon was removed from the atmosphere. Through geologic processes possibly related to plate tectonics, this carbon was carried into the Earth's crust. At present approximately 0.1 percent of the carbon fixed annually is lost to the biosphere in this way. During the Proterozoic (2.5 billion to 542 million years ago), this process allowed some free oxygen to exist in the atmosphere for the first time.

Cyanobacteria were also the first organisms to utilize water as a source of electrons and hydrogen in the photosynthetic process. Free oxygen was released as a result of this reaction and began to accumulate in the atmosphere, allowing oxygen-dependent life-forms to evolve.

THE GROWING COMPLEXITY

Fossils discovered in 1992 in Michigan in the United States suggest that the first eukaryotes appeared about two billion years ago. These complex, single-celled organisms such as amoebas differ from prokaryotes in that they have a membrane-bound nucleus, paired chromosomes, and, in most, mitochondria. They also require oxygen to function.

Major changes in the evolution of the biosphere occurred in the late Precambrian (about 700 to 542 million years ago). Before this time, for about 1.4 billion years following their first appearance, single-celled eukaryotes had been the dominant life-form on the Earth. Then, in the late Precambrian, complex multicellular organisms (animals or plants composed of large numbers of more or less specialized cells) evolved and diversified rapidly.

THE CHALLENGES TO THE DEVELOPMENT OF LIFE

The development of complex life before this time may have been hindered by the atmospheric changes that the biota produced. The prior abundance of carbon dioxide in the atmosphere had provided an insulating, or greenhouse, effect. As organisms removed this gas from the atmosphere, the greenhouse effect was lessened and the Earth's climate changed. This occurrence is believed to have resulted in severe ice ages that gripped the planet.

The causes of the ice ages are still hotly debated. One hypothesis proposed in 1990 by the geologist John James Veevers links their occurrence to continental drift. According to this model, continental drift is cyclic: in the past 1.2 billion years the continents have fluctuated between a phase in which all the Earth's landmasses are

THE GREENHOUSE EFFECT

The greenhouse effect is an expression used to describe the warming of the Earth's surface and troposphere (the lowest layer of the atmosphere), caused by the presence of water vapour, carbon dioxide, methane, and certain other gases in the air. Of these gases, known as greenhouse gases, water vapour has the largest effect.

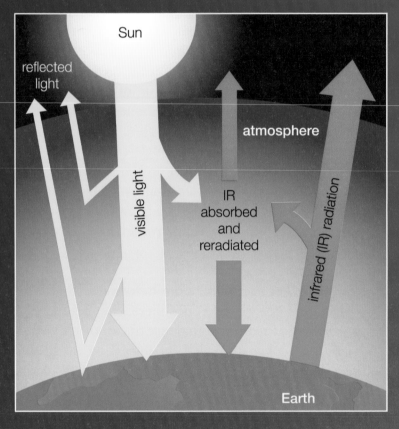

The greenhouse effect on Earth. Some incoming sunlight is reflected by the Earth's atmosphere and surface, but most is absorbed by the surface, which is warmed. Infrared (IR) radiation is then emitted from the surface. Some IR radiation escapes to space, but some is absorbed by the atmosphere's greenhouse gases (especially water vapour, carbon dioxide, and methane) and reradiated in all directions, some to space and some back toward the surface, where it further warms the surface and the lower atmosphere. Encyclopædia Britannica, Inc.

The atmosphere allows most of the visible light from the Sun to pass through and reach the Earth's surface. As the Earth's surface is heated by sunlight, it radiates part of this energy back toward space as infrared radiation. This radiation, unlike visible light, tends to be absorbed by the greenhouse gases in the atmosphere, raising its temperature. The heated atmosphere in turn radiates infrared radiation back toward the Earth's surface. (Despite its name, the greenhouse effect is different from the warming in a greenhouse, where panes of glass transmit visible sunlight but hold heat inside the building by trapping warmed air.)

Without the heating caused by the greenhouse effect, the Earth's average surface temperature would be only about -18 °C (0 °F). On Venus the very high concentration of carbon dioxide in the atmosphere causes an extreme greenhouse effect resulting in surface temperatures as high as 450 °C (840 °F).

Although the greenhouse effect is a naturally occurring phenomenon, it is possible that the effect could be intensified by the emission of greenhouse gases into the atmosphere as the result of human activity. From the beginning of the Industrial Revolution through the end of the 20th century, the amount of carbon dioxide in the atmosphere increased 30 percent and the amount of methane more than doubled. A number of scientists have predicted that human-related increases in atmospheric carbon dioxide and other greenhouse gases could lead to an increase in the global average temperature of 1.4 to 5.8 °C (2.5 to 10.4 °F) by the end of the 21st century. This global warming could alter the Earth's climates and thereby produce new patterns and extremes of drought and rainfall and possibly disrupt food production in certain regions. Other scientists involved in climatic research maintain that such predictions are overstated, however.

separate and a "supercontinent" phase, in which these distinct landmasses formed one continent. During the supercontinent phase, little spreading of the seafloor, with its concomitant release of carbon dioxide from the Earth's mantle, would have occurred. Thus, less carbon dioxide would be present in the atmosphere and the greenhouse effect would be lessened, creating a cooler environment. Major ice ages are believed to coincide with each of the supercontinent phases. (However, the ice ages of the past two million years, which were short-lived and oscillating, are not thought to be part of this larger cycle.)

The distribution of life-forms dependent on a nearby shoreline or a terrestrial habitat has been affected by the relative positions of the continents. The cyclic breakup of supercontinents has provided many opportunities for evolution to continue in isolation. Today Australia is the most isolated of the continents, and its unique flora and fauna are well known. In the past other landmasses have been equally if not more isolated. A part of what is now Central Asia, known as Kazakhstania, was an isolated landmass that existed between the latter half of the Cambrian (beginning about 513 million years ago) and the middle of the Devonian (about 385 million years ago). On these and other landmasses unique floras and faunas evolved.

EXTINCTION AND DIVERSIFICATION

Until the 1980s the fossil record of early multicellular organisms was interpreted to be one of simple and rapid diversification. The paleontologist Adolf Seilacher and others have argued that this is incorrect and that the earliest faunas of multicellular organisms include few or no species that are directly ancestral to later faunas. As evidence they point to the early fauna from the Ediacaran period—animals living at the end of the Precambrian era, between 635 million and 542 million years ago, that were named after the Ediacara Hills in South Australia. Few of the Ediacaran fauna are believed to be related to the later fauna of the Burgess Shale of western Canada (from the middle of the Cambrian [about 520 million to 500 million years ago]). In this view the fossil record is believed to have resulted from at least two more or less independent evolutionary radiations of multicellular organisms followed by severe extinction. Thus extensive extinctions would have played an important role in the evolution of life even at this distant period. Other authorities disagree with this model and maintain that the Ediacaran animals have relatives from the Phanerozoic Era (encompassing the Paleozoic, Mesozoic, and Cenozoic [542 million years ago to the present]), such as sea pens and polychaete worms.

THE CAMBRIAN EXPLOSION

The beginning of the Cambrian Period, now thought to date from 542 million rather than 570 million years ago, witnessed an unparalleled explosion of life. Many of the major phyla that characterize modern animal life—various researchers recognize between 20 and 35—appear to have evolved at that time, possibly over a period of only a few million years. Many other phyla evolved during this time, the great majority of which became extinct during the following 50 million to 100 million years. Ironically, many of the most successful modern phyla (including the chordates, which encompass all vertebrates) are rare elements in Cambrian assemblages; phyla that include the arthropods and sponges contained the most numerically dominant taxa (taxonomic groups) during the Cambrian, and those were the taxa that became extinct.

The beginning of the Cambrian is marked by the evolution of hard parts such as calcium carbonate shells. These body parts fossilize more easily than soft tissues, and thus the fossil record becomes much more complete after their appearance. Many lineages of animals independently evolved hard parts at about the same time. The reasons for this are still debated, but a leading theory is that the amount of oxygen in the atmosphere had finally reached levels that allowed large, complex animals to exist.

Oxygen levels may also have facilitated the metabolic processes that produce collagen, a protein building block that is the basis for hard structures in the body.

Other major changes that occurred in the Early Cambrian (542 million to 510 million years ago) include the development of animal species that burrowed into the sediments of the seafloor, rather than lying on top of it, and the evolution of the first carbonate reefs, which were built by spongelike animals called archaeocyathids.

By the Early Cambrian the biosphere was still restricted to the margins of the world's oceans; no life was found on land (except possibly cyanobacteria [formerly known as blue-green algae] in moist sediment), relatively few pelagic species (biota living in the open sea) existed, and no organisms inhabited the ocean depths. Life in the shallow regions of the seafloor, however, was already well diversified. This early aquatic ecosystem included the relatively large carnivore *Anomalocaris*, the deposit-feeding trilobites (early arthropods) and mollusks, the suspension-feeding sponges, various scavenging arthropods, and possibly even parasites such as the onychophoran *Aysheaia*. Thus, it seems likely that a well-developed aquatic ecosystem was already in operation in the ocean shallows by this time.

Following the Cambrian Period, the biosphere continued to expand relatively rapidly. In the Ordovician Period (488 million to 444 million years ago) the classic Paleozoic marine faunas, which included bryozoans, brachiopods, corals, nautiloids, and crinoids, developed. Many marine species died off near the end of the Ordovician because of environmental changes. The Early Silurian (444 million to 423 million years ago) marks a time when a rapid evolution of many suspension-feeders in the oceans occurred. As a result, pelagic predators such as nautiloids became abundant. Gnathostome fishes, the oldest craniates, became common during the Late Silurian (423 million to 416 million years ago).

THE EMERGENCE OF TERRESTRIAL LIFE

Plants invaded the land in the latter part of the Silurian, about 420 million years ago, and by 410 million years ago various arthropods were found on land. By the middle of the Devonian (about 390 million to 380 million years ago) true spiders capable of spinning silk had evolved. Winged insects followed some 50 million years later. By the Late Devonian (385 million to 359 million years ago) some vertebrates also had emerged onto the land. They were to give rise to the chordates—amphibians, reptiles, birds, and mammals.

Terrestrial plants are believed to have evolved from the chlorophytes, such as the green algae. Their survival on land demanded special adaptations to prevent them from drying out and to aid them in obtaining nutrients and in reproducing. The evolution of cutin, which forms a waxy layer on plants (the cuticle), and stomata helped to prevent desiccation, the development of roots and supporting tissues helped to provide nourishment, and spores and seeds provided means of reproducing.

Fungi were very early partners of the land plants. Mycorrhizal fungi appear to have been associated with the roots of such ancient plants as *Rhynia* (a possible ancestor of ferns), horsetails, and seed plants, while lichenlike plant fragments have been preserved in ancient rocks (lichens are a symbiotic association of fungi and algae).

The earliest widespread land plant that has been preserved, and also the oldest known vascular plant (a plant that possesses specialized tissues, allowing transport

Green algae is believed to be a prime progenitor of the terrestrial plant species evident on Earth today. www.istockphoto.com / Mohamed Sadath

of water and nutrients as well as providing support), is *Cooksonia*. This ancestral plant was mosslike in structure; it has been found in rocks 410 million years old on several continents. *Cooksonia*, or plants similar to it, soon gave rise to all other divisions of vascular plants. Some of the earliest vascular plants include the proto-lycopod *Baragwanathia* and *Rhynia*, both of the Late Silurian to Early Devonian. By the Middle Devonian the development of a cambium and phloem in some plant lineages allowed tree-size species to develop. The giant lycopods, relatives of modern club mosses, were particularly abundant at this time. Seeds or seedlike structures soon followed in a number of plant lineages.

In adapting to life on land, the earliest terrestrial vertebrates faced problems similar to those of the plants. Some members of a group of fleshy-finned, air-breathing fish—the crossopterygians—are believed to have been the ancestors of the land-dwelling vertebrates. *Eusthenopteron* is the best-known of these.

By the Late Devonian the earliest tetrapods had appeared. Forms such as *Ichthyostega* and *Acanthostega* (both from eastern Greenland) are the best-known. Aptly described as fish with legs, they are classified as labyrinthodont amphibians, which retained many fishlike features, including gills, up to eight digits per foot, and a tail fin.

In the Devonian Period a rapid evolution of the fishes occurred; all the major groups appeared or diversified during this time. Among the best-known and most characteristic of the fishes of the period are the placoderms (extinct jawed fishes). Many were heavily armoured species that led a bottom-dwelling existence, while others were pelagic and more lightly scaled. They became extinct at the end of the Devonian.

During the Carboniferous (359 million to 299 million years ago) and Early Permian (299 million to 271 million years ago) the labyrinthodonts became the dominant life-forms, evolving into myriad species. Many lineages became extinct at the close of the Permian (251 million years ago), although at least one held on at high latitudes in the Southern Hemisphere until the Early Cretaceous (146 million to 99.6 million years ago). The lissamphibians, including the frogs and salamanders, made their first undisputed appearance in the fossil record in the Early Triassic (251 million to 246 million years ago).

THE PROGRESSION OF EVOLUTION

Life on Earth is characterized by periods of extinction and species diversification. Continental rearrangements, orbital variations, changes in atmospheric chemistry, extraterrestrial impacts, and other factors contribute to environmental change. Environmental change often upsets ecosystems and threatens the survival of the organisms that inhabit them. If environmental change comes slowly, the extinction rate is relatively low. In some cases, however, the changes are rapid and whole lineages of organisms are lost within a relatively short span of time. In the aftermath of such events, evolution accelerates and new species rise up to assume the roles and occupy the habitats of those that have passed on. Today's world, with its complex array of life-forms and its myriad ecosystems, is the result of several periods of extinction and speciation.

GLACIATION AND DROUGHT DURING THE PERMIAN PERIOD

The interval between the middle of the Carboniferous and the Early Permian is characterized by a prolonged ice age. All the continents were joined into one supercontinent (Pangea), and a vast ice sheet covered what is now

Antarctica, southern Australia, most of India, the southern half of Africa, and much of eastern South America. The giant lycopods, which thrived in the warm swamps of the Devonian and Early Carboniferous (359 million to 318 million years ago), vanished as a result. In their place the now extinct seed ferns of the so-called *Archaeopteris* flora became abundant. On southern continents the Permian is characterized by the dominance of the *Glossopteris* flora. These enigmatic trees and shrubs may have given rise to the major plant groups of the Mesozoic Era (251 million to 65.5 million years ago) and possibly even the flowering plants. By the end of the Permian, gymnosperms (seed plants whose seeds lack a covering) such as ginkgoes and early conifers had appeared. By the Early Triassic they had become widespread in drier environments that other plants could not tolerate.

The close of the Permian is marked by perhaps the greatest well-documented extinction event on the Earth. In all, about 96 percent of the marine species vanished, including the horn and tabulate corals, trilobites, eurypterids, most groups of nautiloids, many echinoderm groups, and many brachiopods and bryozoans. Typical of the extent of the extinctions was the fate of bryozoans. Among the many earlier groups, only one lineage of bryozoans (the cyclostomes) survived the Permian crisis. Bryozoans remained rare until the early Mesozoic, becoming abundant again during the Cretaceous Period (146 million to 65.5 million years ago) and remaining so into modern times. Vertebrates were less affected by this event than invertebrates.

THE REPTILIAN RADIATION

The earliest reptilian fossils have been found in rocks from the Carboniferous, about 340 million years ago.

GYMNOSPERMS

Italian cypress (Cupressus sempervirens). W.H. Hodge

A gymnosperm is any vascular plant that reproduces by means of an exposed seed, or ovule, as opposed to an angiosperm, or flowering plant, whose seeds are enclosed by mature ovaries, or fruits. The seeds of many gymnosperms (literally, "naked seed") are borne in cones and are not visible. These cones, however, are not the same as fruits. During pollination, the immature male gametes, or pollen grains, sift among the cone scales and land directly on the ovules, which contain the immature female gametes, rather than on elements of a flower (the stigma and carpel) as in angiosperms. Furthermore, at maturity, the cone expands to reveal the naked seeds.

It was in 1825 that the Scottish botanist Robert Brown first distinguished gymnosperms from angiosperms. At one time they were considered to be a single class of seed plants, called Gymnospermae, but taxonomists now tend to recognize four distinct divisions (and orders) of extant gymnospermous plants—Pinophyta (order Pinales), Cycadophyta (Cycadales), Ginkgophyta (Ginkgoales), and Gnetophyta (Gnetales)—and to use the term gymnosperms only informally when referring to the naked-seed habit. Not all divisions of gymnosperms are closely related, having been distinct groups for hundreds of millions of years. Currently, 82 genera are recognized, with a total of 947 species. Gymnosperms are distributed throughout the world, with extensive latitudinal and longitudinal ranges.

These early reptiles gave rise to the synapsid reptiles, which became abundant by the Permian. Synapsids were terrestrial predators that included some very large species such as *Dimetrodon*, which had elongated neural spines, forming a "sail" along their backs. One group of synapsids, the therapsids, or mammal-like reptiles, gave rise to mammals in the Late Triassic.

Primitive diapsid reptiles gave rise to two principal groups, the lepidosaurs ("scaly reptiles"), which includes lizards and snakes, and the archosaurs ("ruling reptiles"), which includes dinosaurs and crocodiles. They first appeared in the Late Carboniferous, about 300 million years ago, and for 60 million years afterward they remained small, with generalized characteristics. Only after the great Permian extinction did they begin to diversify and dominate the environment as they gained in size, abundance, and variety.

The Triassic Period (251 million to 200 million years ago) began with relatively warm and wet conditions, but as it progressed conditions became increasingly hot and dry. During this time primitive lepidosaurs flourished; the sphenodontids (of whom the only surviving member is New Zealand's tuatara) were particularly abundant. Lizards were present by the Triassic, while snakes evolved from monitor-like lizards about 120 million years ago during the Early Cretaceous.

The archosaurs dominated terrestrial life from the Middle Triassic (245 million to 228 million years ago) until the end of the Cretaceous. The best-known archosaurs were the dinosaurs, but pterosaurs (flying reptiles), crocodiles, and birds are included in the group.

Birds are believed to have evolved from an order of primitive archosaurs, Thecodontia. The earliest fossil evidence of birds is that of the crow-sized *Archaeopteryx* from the Late Jurassic.

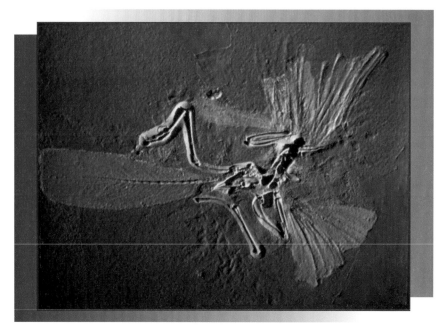

Archaeopteryx skeleton, cast made from a fossil found in limestone matrix.
Courtesy of the American Museum of Natural History, New York

THE DIVERSITY OF CRETACEOUS LIFE

During the Cretaceous Period large dinosaurs such as the predatory *Tyrannosaurus*, the herbivorous *Triceratops*, and the sauropod *Alamosaurus* were dominant forms on land. Marine life included invertebrates such as globigerinid foraminiferans and calcareous radiolarians, which were abundant in the Jurassic Period (200 million to 146 million years ago). Their remains were to coat the ocean floor for the first time with calcareous ooze, which is useful in correlating the age of sedimentary rocks at various locations. Modern groups of mollusks such as clams and carnivorous snails, along with teleost fish (predecessors of most modern fish), all first appeared while plesiosaurs, pliosaurs, and mosasaurs (the last gigantic relatives of goannas) were the major predators. The pterosaurs were the dominant large flying animals. Gymnosperms such as ginkgoes, cycads, and ferns were the dominant plants, although angiosperms became increasingly prevalent toward the end of the period. Birds, which first appeared in the Jurassic, and mammals, which evolved in the Triassic, were also in existence but were minor components of the Earth's fauna, in contrast to their dominance in the Cenozoic Era (65.5 million years ago to the present). It seems likely that various insect groups diversified rapidly at this time in response to the ecological opportunities opened by the spread of flowering plants.

THE EFFECTS OF CLIMATE

The maximum development of greenhouse conditions occurred in the Cretaceous and was probably associated with an increase of greenhouse gases such as carbon dioxide in the atmosphere. There were no polar ice caps during this time, and land within both the Arctic and Antarctic circles was able to support a diversity of plant and animal life. The sea level was considerably higher than at present, and the low-lying parts of the continents formed vast but shallow inland seas. This habitat supported various large bivalves such as the reef-forming rudistid and the metre- (3.3-foot-) long, mussel-like *Inoceramus*.

Studies of newly discovered Cretaceous fauna and flora from the Arctic and Antarctic have revealed interesting differences and some anomalies associated with greenhouse conditions. The Arctic faunas were dominated by large dinosaurs, which are thought to have been migratory. Smaller endothermic animals such as mammals were present, but small ectothermic species such as lizards were not. The Antarctic faunas are strikingly different. Small, herbivorous, bird-hipped dinosaurs such as *Atlascopcosaurus* were the most abundant of the fauna. Turtles and lungfish also were present, while the largest carnivores were the two-metre-high species of *Allosaurus* and the late-surviving labyrinthodonts. The dinosaurs and other Antarctic fauna apparently did not migrate and must have endured several months of near-freezing conditions and total darkness. How they coped remains unclear.

MASS EXTINCTION

The Cretaceous Period came to an abrupt end about 65.5 million years ago with a massive extinction event. Dinosaurs, ammonites and most belemnites (both related to squid and nautiluses), rudist clams, and toothed birds all became extinct. Indeed, all animal species that reached an adult weight of approximately 25 kg (55 pounds) at sexual maturity appear to have disappeared at this time. Smaller organisms such as calcareous plankton, glass sponges, freshwater fish, and brachiopods were severely diminished in diversity, as were gymnosperms and angiosperms of the laurel group.

The cause of this—one of the world's great extinction events—is still hotly debated. Many biological, climatic, and extraterrestrial factors have been put forward to explain it. The asteroid theory, proposed by Walter and Luis Alvarez about 1980, postulates that the extinction was a result of the Earth's collision with an asteroid about 10 to 20 km (about 6 to 12 miles) in diameter. It is generally supposed that the impact caused vast amounts of particulate matter to be emitted into the upper atmosphere, obscuring the Sun and resulting in a drastic reduction in photosynthetic activity and a global cooling.

The asteroid theory has promoted renewed interest in extinctions in general. Some researchers have postulated that extinction events are cyclic, occurring approximately every 26 million years. Although this theory is not widely accepted, there is an emerging consensus that extinction events have been more frequent, more catastrophic, and more variable in effect than was previously realized. It is also becoming apparent that, because they randomly influence the survival or extinction of various species, extinctions are one of the major determinants of evolutionary direction.

THE EARLY PALEOGENE TRANSITION

The evolutionary and ecological responses of species surviving the Cretaceous extinction appear to have been rapid. One surviving species of fern is thought to have covered 90 percent of the land surface of the Earth within 10,000 years of the catastrophe. Various groups, including mammals, birds, flowering plants and their associated insects, barnacles, and bryozoans, diversified rapidly. Differentiation also occurred as flora and fauna were separated by continental shifting.

THE RISE OF THE MAMMALS

Among the three groups of modern mammals, egg-laying monotremes and marsupials have persisted in relatively small numbers and have been most successful on the southern continents. The monotremes are the most primitive of living mammals, and only two types have survived—the duck-billed platypus and the echidnas. The third mammalian group, the placental mammals, has met with the greatest success, giving rise to flying forms (bats), marine species (whales, sirenians, and seals), and an extraordinary variety of land-based forms.

The diversification of the placental mammals was rapid. A few million years after the extinction of the dinosaurs during the Paleogene Period (65.5 million to 23 million years ago), some placental groups such as the

A baby duck-billed platypus makes his debut at an Australian zoo. These curious-looking creatures are one of only two existing monotremes, which are the earliest known mammals. Greg Wood/AFP/Getty Images

arctocyonid plant-eaters (which gave rise to the ungulates) had quadrupled their number of species. The placentals also increased in size and ecological range. At the time of the Cretaceous extinction the largest placentals were no larger than a cat. By the end of the Paleocene Epoch (65.5 million to 55.8 million years ago), about 10 million years later, species weighing more than 800 kg (about 1,760 pounds) had evolved. By this time mammals had diversified to fill the major ecological niches, including those of large herbivores, carnivores, scavengers, and more specialized types. Thus during the Paleocene the most rapid evolution of mammal genera and families occurred. The flowering plants and their associated insects expanded rapidly during the rest of the Cenozoic Era as well. They also differentiated into distinct floras and faunas following their isolation on the various continents.

THE EMERGENCE OF THE PRIMATES

Among the placental mammals to appear during the Late Cretaceous were the primates. A small group of large-bodied, tailless species—the apes—eventually diverged to give rise to a bipedal lineage about 3.5 million years ago. The genus *Homo* evolved from this line 2 million years ago. Between 200,000 and 100,000 years ago modern humans, *Homo sapiens*, had evolved; they are believed to have left their Afro-Eurasian homeland for the first time, invading Australasia about 40,000 years ago. By 11,000 years ago they had entered the Americas, thus completing their colonization of the habitable continents.

CENOZOIC CLIMATIC FLUCTUATIONS

The period of time following the Late Cretaceous extinction event, the Cenozoic Era (65.5 million years ago to the present), was marked by climatic fluctuations with a general trend toward cooling. The Early Eocene (55.8 million to 48.6 million years ago) was warm; however, by the end of the Eocene (33.9 million years ago) the world experienced an abrupt drop in temperature. At the beginning of the Miocene (23.03 million years ago) warmer conditions returned, only to disappear by the end of the epoch (5.33 million years ago). Since then the climate has oscillated, culminating about 2.4 million years ago in the onset of the ice ages, with many advances and retreats of the world's ice caps.

In the latter part of the Eocene (about 40 million years ago) Antarctica had begun to develop significant snowfields and associated glaciers, the first to appear on the continent since the Permian. An ice cap had developed by 16.5 million to 13 million years ago, with its most rapid development occurring between 14.8 million and 14 million years ago. By 6 million years ago a vast ice cap had finally linked East and West Antarctica.

The Effects of Aquatic Changes

In the latter Eocene the temperature of the bottom water of the southern ocean dropped dramatically, by 4 to 5 °C (7 to 9 °F). This appears to have been caused by the increasing physical, and thus thermal, isolation of Antarctica and its surrounding seas. The isolation was completed with the opening of the Drake Passage between Antarctica and South America and the establishment of the Antarctic Circumpolar Current sometime before the Early Miocene (23.03 million to 15.97 million years ago). This ultimately led to the development of the Antarctic Bottom Water—cold, deep, nutrient-rich water that today originates at Antarctica and flows north to all the major oceans of the world. The development of the Antarctic Bottom Water has had a profound effect on life in the oceans owing to its novel nutrient-carrying capacity. Because of this ability, it is believed to have led to major changes in nutrient cycling when it was first established. It may, for example, be responsible for the abundance of krill and thus for the evolution of the great mysticete (filter-feeding) whales, which first appeared in the Oligocene (33.9 million to 23.03 million years ago).

Glacial Periods

The development of an extensive ice cap in Antarctica six million years ago led to a dramatic fall in sea level. At its height, the terminal Miocene ice age saw Antarctica's Ross Ice Shelf extend about 300 to 400 km (about 190 to 250 miles) north of its present position. This event isolated the Mediterranean Sea, which experienced numerous cycles of evaporation and refilling during subsequent oscillations in temperature. As a consequence of these changes, approximately one million cubic km (about 240,000 cubic miles) of salt and gypsum were removed from the world's oceans and now lie buried in sedimentary deposits below the Mediterranean Sea. These events left the world's oceans approximately 6 percent less salty than before. This in turn contributed to the cooling of the global climate, because the reduced salinity raised the freezing point of the oceans. This promoted the formation of high-latitude sea ice and also enhanced the reflectivity of the Earth's surface (albedo).

The ice ages of the Late Miocene (11.61 million to 5.33 million years ago) and Pleistocene appear to have been caused by events different from those of earlier ice ages, such as those of the Carboniferous and Early Permian. Variations in the tilt and precession, or wobble, of the Earth's axis and in the shape of the Earth's orbit are thought to be responsible for the more recent ice ages, which recur approximately every 100,000 years.

QUATERNARY EXTINCTIONS

During the Pleistocene the diversification of mammals continued, accompanied by localized and fewer widespread extinction events. In the terminal Pleistocene (50,000 to 10,000 years ago), however, extinction events occurred without a large number of groups of larger vertebrates being replaced. The species that became extinct, which included mammoths, mastodons, ground sloths, and giant beavers, are collectively known as megafauna. The late Pleistocene extinction of megafauna did not occur synchronously nor was it of equal magnitude throughout the world.

Considerable doubt exists regarding the timing of the megafaunal extinctions on various landmasses. Currently, evidence suggesting that the earliest mass megafaunal extinctions occurred in Australia and New Guinea about 30,000 or more years ago is emerging. During this time large marsupials such as diprotodons, reptiles such as the seven-metre-long goanna, *Megalania*, and large flightless birds vanished. Eighty-six percent of the Australian vertebrate genera whose members weighed more than 40 kg (about 90 pounds) became extinct.

Much smaller extinction events occurred in Africa, Asia, and Europe earlier in the Pleistocene, removing very large species such as rhinoceroses, elephants, and the largest artiodactyls. Other mass megafaunal extinction events occurred on the Eurasian tundra about 12,000 years ago (affecting mammoths, Irish elk, and woolly rhinoceroses); in North and South America they occurred about 11,000 years ago (affecting a wide variety of species, including elephants, giant sloths, lions, and bears). These extinctions have removed 29 percent of the vertebrate genera weighing more than 40 kg from Europe and 73 percent of such genera from North America.

Until 1,000 to 2,000 years ago the megafauna of large, long-isolated landmasses such as New Zealand and Madagascar survived. Gigantic birds such as the elephant birds of Madagascar and the moas of New Zealand disappeared after the Pleistocene in the past few thousand years.

The causes of the extinctions of the late Pleistocene are still debated; however, there is widespread agreement that the arrival of humans heralded the most recent extinction events in New Zealand and Madagascar. Earlier events are less well understood, with researchers divided between whether human-induced change or an alteration in the climate was the principal cause.

Recently the effects of megafaunal extinction on vegetation and climate, particularly in Australia, have received attention. Australian megafaunal extinction, followed by an increase in the incidence of fire, may have led to structural changes in vegetation, which resulted in decreased effective precipitation, more impoverished soils, and even the failure of Lake Eyre to fill during otherwise favourable conditions.

The past 10,000 years have seen dramatic changes in the biosphere. The invention of agriculture and animal husbandry and the eventual spread of these practices throughout the world have allowed humans to co-opt a large portion of the available productivity of the Earth. Calculations show that humans currently use approximately 40 percent of the energy of the Sun captured by organisms on land. Use of such an inordinately large proportion of the Earth's productivity by a single animal species is unique in the history of the planet.

The human population continues to expand at the rate of approximately 80 million persons per year and may reach 10 billion sometime in the 21st century. Changes to the atmosphere caused by complex technology and the increasing population threaten to cause major disruptions to the biosphere. Among the most important changes is the release of greenhouse gases — including carbon dioxide, methane, and chlorofluorocarbons — into the atmosphere.

Despite the enormous advances made in understanding the biosphere over the past few decades, there is clearly much more to learn. Many would agree that we are just beginning to perceive the complex process that keeps the biosphere hospitable to life.

CHAPTER 3
BIOMES AND ECOSYSTEMS

The largest of Earth's ecological communities are biomes and biogeographic regions. Each one of these vast systems possesses a unique set of species and climatic conditions. However, noticeable patterns emerge. Deserts around the world are characterized by high atmospheric pressure and low moisture, whereas tropical rainforests on different continents have ample moisture and warm temperatures. These climatic conditions contribute to the dominant vegetation type found in each area. (Deserts are characterized by sparse, shrubby vegetation, whereas tropical forests are made up of a rich diversity of thick-canopied tall trees.) This chapter is devoted to describing the unique characteristics of different biomes and biogeographic regions, as well as the features some share with others.

A biogeographic region is an area of animal and plant distribution having similar or shared characteristics throughout. It is a matter of general experience that the plants and animals of the land and inland waters differ to a greater or lesser degree from one part of the world to another. Why should this be? Why should the same species not exist wherever suitable environmental conditions for them prevail?

Geographic regions around the world that have similar environmental conditions are capable of harbouring the same type of biota. This situation effectively separates the biosphere into biomes—ecological communities that have the same climatic conditions and geologic features and that support species with similar life strategies and adaptations. A biome is frequently described as a major community of plants and animals with similar life-forms and environmental conditions. It includes various communities and is named for the dominant type of vegetation, such as grassland or coniferous forest. Several similar biomes constitute a biome type—for example, the temperate deciduous forest biome type includes the deciduous forest biomes of Asia, Europe, and North America. "Major life zone" is the European phrase for the North American biome concept.

The biome is the fundamental unit of which larger biogeographic regions (floral kingdoms and faunal realms) consist. The tropical forest is one type of terrestrial biome. It is located at various points around the planet where climatic and geologic conditions produce similar environments. The tropical forest biome contains the same general kinds of biological communities wherever it occurs. However, the individual species will not be the same from one tropical forest to another. Instead, each forest will support organisms that are ecologically equivalent—i.e., different species that have a similar life cycle and have adapted analogously to environmental conditions.

How the unique distributions of animals and plants in various biomes came to be is not explicable purely through present climatic factors and latitudinal zonation. Geologic events such as continental drift and past climatic conditions must be taken into consideration as well. This is the approach used in historical biogeography to study the distributions of flora and fauna throughout the world.

THE CONCEPT OF BIOGEOGRAPHY

Biogeography, the study of animal and plant distributions (and known individually as zoogeography and phytogeography, respectively), was a subject that began to receive much attention in the 19th century. One of the first modern delimitations of biogeographic regions was created in

Early studies regarding biogeographic delimitations influenced the work of Charles Darwin, who was a pioneer in the field of evolution. Spencer Arnold/Hulton Archive/Getty Images

1858 by the English ornithologist Philip L. Sclater, who based his division of the terrestrial world on the distributions of birds. In the 1870s the biologist Adolf Engler devised a schema based on plant distributions.

The phytogeographic work of Sir Joseph Dalton Hooker, a plant collector and systematist, and the zoogeographic work of Alfred Russel Wallace greatly influenced the work of Charles Darwin. The Darwinian theory of evolution, accordingly, was firmly rooted in the emerging biogeographic understanding of the era. In *On the Origin of Species* Darwin included two key chapters (12 and 13) on geographic distribution in which he referred to both Hooker and Wallace. At high altitudes in the tropics Hooker had found plants that were normally restricted to temperate zones, and Darwin interpreted these observations as evidence of past climatic change. Darwin also adopted Wallace's view of faunal distribution among islands: those islands exhibiting similar faunas are separated only by shallow water and were once a contiguous landmass that presented no barrier to animal dispersal, whereas those islands whose faunas are dissimilar are separated by deep seaways that have always existed and barred the migration of species.

BIOTIC DISTRIBUTIONS

Geographic factors have played a significant role at every level of taxonomic division. Populations that become isolated by means of a geographic barrier will tend to diverge from their species. Although these barriers — which include seaways, rivers, mountain ranges, deserts, and other hostile environments — appear minor, they nevertheless can put a wedge between taxa, eventually causing related species, genera, families, and so on (on up the taxonomic hierarchy) to diverge. An example of this mechanism is seen in the Gregory Rift Valley, the eastern branch of the East African Rift System; distinctive sub-species of wildebeest are represented on either side of the rift valley, with the subspecies *Connochaetes taurinus albojubatus* occurring on the east side and *C.t. hecki* on the west. Other mammals such as blue, or diadem, monkeys (*Cercopithecus mitis*) exhibit similar geographic variation. The broad Congo River in central Africa is a barrier between many congeneric species (those that share the same genus) of primates, such as the common chimpan-zee (*Pan troglodytes*) found on the north side of the river and the pygmy chimpanzee (*P. paniscus*), or bonobo, living to the south of the river. More significant biogeographic divisions occur between genera of the same family that live on different continents, as is the case with African elephants (*Loxodonta*) and Asian elephants (*Elephas*). Whole families or suborders may differ from one major biogeographic realm to another, as is seen in the primate divisions of Old World monkeys (catarrhines), which are found in Africa and Asia, and the New World monkeys (platyrrhines) from South America.

DISPERSALIST AND VICARIANCE BIOGEOGRAPHY

Within historical biogeography, two views—the dispersal-ist and vicariance hypotheses of biotic distribution patterns—have been at odds. According to the dispersal-ist view, speciation occurs as animals spread out from a centre of origin, crossing preexisting barriers that they would not readily recross and that would cut them off from the original group. The vicariance explanation states that a species that is present over a wide area becomes fragmented (vicariated) as a barrier develops, as occurred through the process of continental drift. These patterns, however, are not mutually exclusive, and both provide insight into the modes of biogeographic distribution. Traditionally biogeographers — and of these mainly zoogeographers such as William Diller Matthew, George Gaylord Simpson, and Philip J. Darlington, Jr. — accepted a number of explanations for the modes of species distribution and differentiation that generally fell into a dispersalist view.

In a series of works from the 1950s and '60s the maverick Venezuelan phytogeographer Leon Croizat strongly objected to this dispersalist explanation of species distribution, which he interpreted as ad hoc events used to explain the geographic distribution of living organisms. He maintained that the regularity in biogeographic relationships was too great to be explained by the chance crossings of barriers. In the 1970s his works sparked the development of the theory of vicarianism.

In spite of the polarization of these views among biogeographers, patterns of distribution can be explained by a combination of dispersalist and vicariance biogeography. Many biogeographers believe that the vicariance process forms the underlying mechanism of distributional diversity, with the dispersalist mode operating more sporadically.

ENDEMISM

A taxon whose distribution is confined to a given area is said to be endemic to that area. The taxon may be of any rank, although it is usually at a family level or below, and its range of distribution may be wide, spanning an entire continent, or very narrow, covering only a few square metres: a species of squirrel (*Sciurus kaibabensis*) is endemic to the Kaibab Plateau in Arizona (U.S.), the primate family Lemuridae is endemic to Madagascar, and the mammalian subclass Prototheria (monotremes) is endemic to the

LAND BRIDGE

Land bridges are any of several isthmuses that have connected the Earth's major landmasses at various times, with the result that many species of plants and animals have extended their ranges to new areas. A land bridge that had a profound effect on the fauna of the New World extended from Siberia to Alaska during most of the Paleogene, Neogene, and Quaternary periods (beginning approximately 65.5 million years ago), with some interruptions. Across this strip of land passed a number of organisms of Old World origin, including *Homo sapiens*.

Another important land bridge, the Isthmus of Panama, was submerged during most of the Paleogene and Neogene, with the result that the faunas of North and South America evolved largely separately, except during the Pliocene Epoch (from about 5.3 million to 2.6 million years ago) for periods of several hundred thousand years, when the isthmus was elevated.

Notogaean (Australian) realm. A distinction is often made between neoendemics (taxa of low rank [e.g., species] that have not had time to spread beyond their region of origin) and paleoendemics (taxa of high rank [e.g., class] that have not yet died out).

The concept of endemism is important because in the past the formulation of biogeographic regions was based on it. The limits of a region are determined by mapping the distributions of taxa; where the outer boundaries of many taxa occur, a line delimiting a biogeographic region is drawn. Major regions (kingdoms and realms) are still determined as those that have the most endemics or, stated another way, those that share the fewest taxa with other regions. As regions are further broken down into subdivisions, they will contain fewer unique taxa.

This method has been criticized because it assumes that species ranges are stable, which they are not. An alternative method of determining biogeographic regions involves calculating degrees of similarity between geographic regions. Similarities of regions can be quantified using Jaccard's coefficient of biotic similarity, which is determined by the equation:

$$s = \frac{c}{a + b + c}.$$

If two areas are being compared, the coefficient of similarity, s, is determined by dividing the number of taxa shared between the areas, c, by the sum of c and the number of taxa peculiar to each area alone, a and b. The larger the coefficient, the more dissimilar are the areas.

COMPONENTS OF SPECIES DIVERSITY

Species diversity is determined not only by the number of species within a biological community—i.e., species richness—but also by the relative abundance of individuals in that community. Species abundance is the number of individuals per species, and relative abundance refers to the evenness of distribution of individuals among species in a community. Two communities may be equally rich in species but differ in relative abundance. For example, each community may contain 5 species and 300 individuals, but in one community all species are equally common (e.g., 60 individuals of each species), while in the second community one species significantly outnumbers the other four.

These components of species diversity respond differently to various environmental conditions. A region that does not have a wide variety of habitats usually is species-poor; however, the few species that are able to occupy the region may be abundant because competition with other species for resources will be reduced.

Trends in species richness may reveal a good deal about both past and present conditions of a region. The Antarctic continent has few species because its environment is so inhospitable; however, oceanic islands are species-poor because they are hard to reach, or, as is the case with the Lesser Sunda Islands in south-central Indonesia, because they are of rather recent origin and organisms have not had enough time to establish themselves.

Global gradients also affect species richness. The most obvious gradient is latitudinal: there are more species in the tropics than in the temperate or polar zones. Ecological factors commonly are used to account for this gradation. Higher temperatures, greater climate predictability, and longer growing seasons all conspire to create a more inviting habitat, permitting a greater diversity of species. Tropical rainforests are the richest habitat of all, tropical grasslands exhibit more diversity than temperate

The golden-headed lion tamarin and grey-winged trumpeter (pictured in a London Zoo exhibit) are just two faunal species that call the tropical rainforest home. Rainforests have the greatest diversity of any ecosystem. Oli Scarff/ Getty Images

grasslands, and deserts in tropical or subtropical regions are populated by a wider range of species than are temperate deserts.

Another factor affecting the species richness of a given area is the distance or barrier that separates the area from potential sources of species. The probability that species will reach remote oceanic islands or isolated valleys is slight. Animal species, especially those that do not fly, are less likely than plant species to do so. The islands of the Lesser Sundas are similar to eastern Java in climate and vegetation, but they have far fewer strictly terrestrial animals. This situation is attributed to the fact that, whereas Java has been connected to a larger landmass in the past, the Lesser Sundas have not. While plants and seeds have been blown across intervening seas, few species of animals that do not have wings have reached these islands.

SPECIES ADAPTATIONS TO CHANGING ENVIRONMENTS

Neither an environment nor an organism is a static entity. Hence, changes in either will disrupt the relationship that has evolved between the two. Small changes in an organism may actually improve the interaction—a random genetic mutation allowing a plant to utilize a nutrient that has been present but previously unusable by the plant will increase the organism's ability to survive. Changes of an extreme nature, however, are almost always maladaptive. Small environmental variations may present a challenge that organisms can meet by mounting a physiological response or, if they are mobile, by removing themselves to a less stressful area. Catastrophic disruptions, however, may create an environment no longer hospitable to the organisms, and they may die out as a result.

Although the distribution patterns of species are dictated by environmental conditions, the actual range of a species is not identical to its potential range—namely, the area that is ecologically compatible with its needs. For example, the biogeographic regions of the world are related to climatic factors, but they are not coterminous with them. Thus, desert biomes, which are located at latitudes of 30° N and S, and tropical rainforest biomes, which arise around the Equator, can be found in most phytogeographic kingdoms and zoogeographic realms.

THE EFFECTS OF GEOLOGIC CHANGES ON BIOTIC DISTRIBUTIONS

The theory of plate tectonics, formulated in the 1960s, is now firmly established. Its explanation of the dynamic nature of continental landmasses has been important not only within the field of geology but also within the field of biogeography; it has entirely revolutionized the interpretation of the dispersal of flora and fauna. The slow movement of continents has been used to explain both the isolation and intermingling of populations. Prior to the acceptance of this idea, land bridges and sunken continents were invoked as the means by which continents were linked in the geologic past. While land bridges, such as the Bering Strait land bridge that connected western North America to Asia, have existed and contributed to the dispersal of organisms, they no longer are believed to have been as ubiquitous and instrumental in this process as once was thought. Such hypothetical land bridges as Archhelenis, which purportedly connected South America and southwestern Africa, are now regarded by most experts as relics of the fertile imaginations of early biogeographers.

During much of the Mesozoic Era (251 million to 65.5 million years ago), the continents formed a single mass that has been named Pangea. In the Early Cretaceous Epoch (145.5 million to 99.6 million years ago), the Tethys seaway formed and split Pangea into a northern continent, Laurasia (encompassing Eurasia and North America), and a southern continent, Gondwanaland (including South America, Antarctica, Africa, India, and Australia). Notwithstanding transient and shifting epicontinental seaways, flora and fauna essentially were able to move freely within the Northern and Southern hemispheres but not between them. During the Late Cretaceous and throughout much of the Cenozoic, Gondwanaland split up and its component parts drifted apart, some of them forming connections with Laurasia, which remained more or less a continuous landmass. According to this model, Australia has remained separate from other continents since the Eocene Epoch (55.8 million to 33.9 million years ago) and had been in contact only with an already polar Antarctica from the Late Cretaceous onward, which helps to explain its remarkably distinct flora and fauna. The life-forms of South America are only less distinctive than those of Australia. Separated from other continents since the Eocene, South America did not have a permanently established connection with North America until the Pliocene (5.3 million to 2.6 million years ago). Only then was some interchange, especially of faunas, permitted. Africa had achieved proximity to Laurasia by the Paleocene Epoch (65.5 million to 55.8 million years ago) and has remained in tenuous connection to Eurasia ever since, so that its present flora and fauna are much more similar to the rest of the Old World tropics. India had formed a broad connection with Laurasia in the Paleogene Period and so has no strongly distinctive (paleoendemic) organisms.

THE DISTRIBUTION BOUNDARIES OF FLORA AND FAUNA

In the past, classifying the flora and fauna into regions was primarily a descriptive event. Today, however, biogeographic classification, like biological taxonomy, is not an end in itself but rather a means to understanding the causative factors involved in evolution, whether they be the vicissitudes of geologic events or the dynamics of biological adaptation. In this sense a classification is not right or wrong so much as it is useful or not.

The sorting of animals and plants into major biogeographic regions is a useful, hypothesis-generating activity. When two taxa of organisms show similar variations in distribution, it is theorized that they have been subject to the same kinds of evolutionary processes, such as ecological constraints that favour certain adaptations or random geographic changes. In a survey of many taxa in a biological community, all may have similar distributional patterns; they may have been restrained by the same geographic barriers or been influenced similarly by climatic factors. When comparing the phytogeographic kingdoms with the zoogeographic realms, one is struck by both the broad agreement in outlines and the differences in details.

Curious discrepancies in these patterns do exist. Some organisms have been able to "skip over" climatic zones so that they are found in both northern and southern temperate zones but not in the intervening tropics. Others appear to have exceptional abilities to disperse to remote, isolated regions and survive. For example, members of the bird family Rallidae (rail) have dispersed throughout many islands, including New Caledonia, Lord Howe Island, Guam, and even the aptly named Inaccessible Island, and the giant tortoises (*Geochelone*) are found on the Galapagos

Islands off the west coast of South America as well as on Seychelles off the east coast of Africa.

Discrepancies also exist between animal and plant distributions. For example, a separate kingdom, the South African (Capensic) kingdom, is recognized for plants but not for animals. In New Guinea the flora is classified in the Paleotropical kingdom, but the fauna is not considered to be of the corresponding Paleotropical realm and instead is classified in the Notogaean realm. Some of these discrepancies are more comprehensible than others. The lack of a faunal Capensic division may simply be a function of the greater mobility of animals. Such divisions, if they ever did exist within zoogeography, have been "swallowed up" by the surrounding Neogaean and Afrotropical faunas. Other differences, especially that of the flora and fauna of New Guinea, are less explicable.

Land and freshwater plant groups are older than the groups of animals with which they coexist; thus, the major phytogeographic regions reflect a more ancient phase in Earth history than do the zoogeographic regions. Because plants are less mobile, their associations have survived into the present relatively intact. The division of the major regions into minor subdivisions helps to elucidate more recent events in Earth history as well as the dispersal capabilities, adaptive strategies, and ecological relationships of the biota.

The importance of the climate's influence on biotic dispersal must not be overlooked. Marine organisms tend to be distributed along climatic lines, and many terrestrial groups, such as migratory birds, are so mobile that they have become spread across two or more major biogeographic areas. Although they are widely dispersed, they have specialized within northern and southern temperate zones, which are separated by the unsuitable tropical regions between.

These odd, disjunct distributions serve as reminders that biogeographic regions only sketch the outlines of organismal distributions and that they do not explain every case. What they are useful for is to point toward dispersal mechanisms, past climatic corridors, and other important biological phenomena.

THE FLORAL KINGDOMS

Six floral kingdoms—Boreal (Holarctic), Paleotropical, Neotropical, South African (Capensic), Australian, and Antarctic—are commonly distinguished. These kingdoms are further broken down into subkingdoms and regions, over which there is some dispute. The kingdoms are not sharply delineated, and the families of higher plants vary in the degree to which they are found across the phytogeographic kingdoms, with their distribution being only partly dependent on their age. The following arrangement is based on the work of Ronald Good (1974).

A GEOGRAPHIC BREAKDOWN OF THE BOREAL KINGDOM

The Boreal, or Holarctic, kingdom consists of Eurasia and North America, which essentially have been a contiguous mass since the Eocene Epoch (55.8 million to 33.9 million years ago). The narrow Bering Strait, between Siberia and Alaska, has existed only since the end of the Pleistocene (some 11,700 years ago). It is no surprise that the differences between the floras of these two continents are minor. Families such as Betulaceae (birch), Brassicaceae (also called Cruciferae), Primulaceae (primrose), Saxifragaceae (saxifrage), Rosaceae (rose), Ranunculaceae (buttercup), and Apiaceae (also called Umbelliferae) are spread across the temperate zone of the Northern Hemisphere. The Boreal kingdom is divided into six regions.

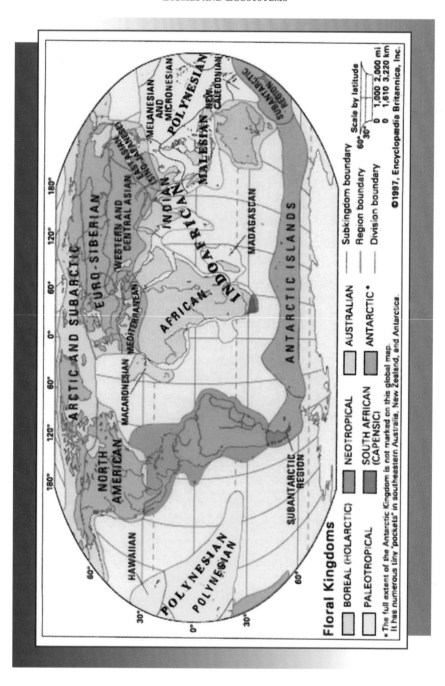

The floral kingdoms of the world. *Copyright Encyclopaedia Britannica; rendering for this edition by Rosen Educational Services.*

The Arctic and subarctic region is the boreal tundra zone, extending from Spitsbergen (an island in the Arctic Ocean to the north of Norway) around the shores of the Arctic Ocean through Siberia and Arctic North America to Greenland. Flowering plants in this region are poor in diversity, but cryptogams are more diverse.

The East Asian, or Sino-Japanese, region, which has about 300 endemic genera, extends from the slopes of the eastern Himalayas into northeastern China and the Russian Far East, including Taiwan, Japan, and Sakhalin Island. In this region, tropical rainforest to the south merges into deciduous forest to the north. Characteristic plant families are Lauraceae (laurel), Magnoliaceae (magnolia), and Theaceae (tea). There are numerous endemic genera; *Berberis*, *Rhododendron*, and *Juniperus* are characteristic mountain genera.

Centred on the desert steppes of Central Asia and Mongolia, the Western and Central Asian region is a floristic zone consisting of 200 or more endemic genera. It extends from the Caucasus to the Plateau of Tibet, with arid zone plants of the family Chenopodiaceae (goosefoot) and genera such as *Salix* (willow), *Astragalus* (milk vetch), and *Picea* (spruce).

The Mediterranean region is the winter rainfall zone of the Holarctic kingdom. It is characterized by sclerophyllous plants mainly of the scrubland type known as maquis. It is difficult to define, however, because many of its characteristic plants (about 250 genera) are centred around but not confined to this region. The region extends entirely around the Mediterranean, from Portugal to Syria. Some classifications place the Canary Islands, which contain a subtropical rainforest biome, in this region, but Good categorizes these islands with the other eastern Atlantic island groups in a separate Macaronesian region, which contains about 30 endemic genera.

The Eurosiberian region extends from Iceland around most of Europe via Siberia to Kamchatka. Conifers of the family Pinaceae—*Pinus* (pine), *Larix* (larch), *Picea*, and *Abies* (fir)—grow in vast, monospecific stands and give way to temperate deciduous forest to the south, tundra to the north, and moorlands (which contain Ericaceae [heath family], *Carex* [sedge], and *Sphagnum* moss in suitable areas). The western part of the region is much richer in species than the eastern part: there are about 100 genera that are endemic to Europe, with only about 12 endemic to Siberia.

The vegetation to the east of the Bering Strait, in the North American region, closely resembles that to the west, in the Eurosiberian region, with slight variations. The conifer genera *Tsuga* (hemlock), *Sequoia* (redwood), and others replace their Eurosiberian counterparts, and there are nine endemic families of flowering plants. Good and others separate the eastern (Atlantic) and western (Pacific) halves of North America into distinct regions, with 100 genera endemic to the Atlantic region and 300 endemic to the Pacific, although these endemic taxa comprise only a small part of the total flora.

THE PALEOTROPICAL KINGDOM AND ITS SUBKINGDOMS

This kingdom extends from Africa, excluding strips along the northern and southern edges, through the Arabian peninsula, India, and Southeast Asia eastward into the Pacific. Plant families that extend over much of the region include the families Pandanaceae (screw pine) and Nepenthaceae (East Indian pitcher plant). The flora in this huge region, however, is not homogenous: 98 percent of species of Hawaiian flora are endemic, as are 70 percent of Fijian floral species and 60 percent of the floral species of New Caledonia. The divisions of the kingdom are disputed, but those most commonly recognized are the Malesian, Indoafrican, and Polynesian subkingdoms.

The Malesian subkingdom encompasses the islands of Southeast Asia and the Malay Peninsula, extending as far east as the mainland of New Guinea. Although it had sometimes been included with India in an Indo-Malayan region, the flora of what C.G.G.J. van Steenis (1950) called Malesia forms a tight-knit unity that can be subdivided into three divisions: a western area covering the Malay Peninsula, Sumatra, Borneo, and the Philippines; a southern area of Java and the Lesser Sundas; and an eastern area of Celebes, the Moluccas, and New Guinea. The region boasts approximately 400 endemic genera (20 percent of the total flora of the Earth), of which 130 genera are found in the western division, 15 in the southern division, and 150 in the eastern division. The biome types range from tropical rainforest to montane and cloud forest, with drier biome types in areas of the southern division. The rainforest biomes in the western part of the region are characterized by the dominance of the family Dipterocarpaceae, although the Guttiferae, Moraceae (mulberry), and Annonaceae (custard apple) families also are found throughout.

In the Indoafrican subkingdom, curiously little distinction is to be made between the flora of Africa (south of the Sahara) and the Indian subcontinent, Myanmar (Burma), and southern China. These areas are narrowly connected by a corridor running through the Arabian Peninsula and southern Iran. The flora of the island of Madagascar is the most divergent in the region and is often regarded as forming a separate region; the island has 12 endemic families and 350 endemic genera, although these form only about a quarter of the total. The flora of Sri Lanka has almost as much in common with Malesia as it does with India. Vegetation ranges from rainforest to semiarid steppe. The families Leguminoseae (legume) and Asteraceae (aster), often called Compositae, achieve their greatest diversity in the region, together with Combretaceae (Indian almond) and, in the arid south of Madagascar, Didiereaceae. Characteristic genera include the grasses *Andropogon* and *Panicum* and the giant baobab (*Adansonia*). In the montane (Afroalpine) zones *Lobelia*, *Senecio*, and *Erica* (heath) are characteristic. About 50 endemic genera define a desert zone extending from the Sahara to northwestern India; 500 are endemic to tropical Africa, 120 to India, and 300 to continental Southeast Asia, but the boundaries of these zones are poorly defined and the distributions of the endemics are only weakly coterminous.

In many respects the Pacific islands are outliers of Malesia, but each of the four main divisions within the Polynesian subkingdom—Hawaii; the remaining portion of Polynesia; Melanesia and Micronesia; and New Caledonia, with Lord Howe and Norfolk islands—has a high number of endemic taxa. Hawaii has more than 40 endemic genera; Polynesia, excluding Hawaii, has almost 20; the division of Melanesia and Micronesia has 38, with 17 confined to Fiji; and New Caledonia has 135 among a total of 600 genera native to the island. Only 21 of the subkingdom's endemic genera occur in more than one of the four divisions. The unbalanced aspect of the flora is illustrated by the dominance, among the endemics, of the Arecaceae family, sometimes called Palmae—there are more than 35 endemic genera of palms in the Polynesian subkingdom—and a few other families.

THE NEOTROPICAL KINGDOM

Essentially the Neotropical kingdom covers all but the extreme southern tip and southwestern strip of South America; Central America; Mexico, excluding the dry north and centre; and beyond to the West Indies and the southern tip of Florida. The vegetation ranges from tropical rainforest in the Amazon and Orinoco basins to open savanna in Venezuela (the Llanos) and Argentina (the Pampas). Forty-seven families and nearly 3,000 genera of flowering plants are endemic to this kingdom; some families, including Bromeliaceae (pineapple) and Cactaceae (cactus), are virtually confined to this kingdom. Within the kingdom, Central America, which includes Mexico and the isthmus, the West Indies, the Venezuela-Guyana region, Brazil, the Andes, and the Pampas all have some measure of endemicity. Although impoverished, the Juan Fernández Islands and the Desventurados Islands, located off the west coast of Chile, exhibit a high endemicity with a general Neotropical affinity.

THE SOUTH AFRICAN KINGDOM

The South African, or Capensic, kingdom consists of the southern and southwestern tip of Africa, the area around the Cape of Good Hope (hence, the designation "Capensic"). It is remarkably rich in plants; 11 families and 500 genera are endemic. This is the smallest of the phytogeographic kingdoms. The winter rainfall climatic regime mimics that of the Mediterranean region, and the general aspect of the vegetation is akin to the scrubland vegetation (maquis) of that region. At the edges of this tiny, restricted zone, the flora merges into the typical flora of Africa—Paleotropical.

THE AUSTRALIAN KINGDOM

The continent of Australia forms a kingdom sharply distinct from the Paleotropic. Rainforest biomes—from tropical in the north that include monsoon forests to temperate in the far south, especially Tasmania—occur along the eastern seaboard. Woodlands of *Eucalyptus* cover much of the eastern third of the continent, and a mosaic of remarkable temperate forests and *Banksia* heathland are found in the southwest. (These two elements of Australian flora, while conspicuous, are not endemic; there are a few species of *Eucalyptus* in eastern New Guinea, New Britain, the Lesser Sundas, and the Philippines, and one species of *Banksia* is found in New Guinea.) Otherwise much of the vegetation is semiarid or adapted to the dryness. About 19 families and 500 genera are endemic. Only the tropical rainforests of northeastern Queensland have a mixed flora, with a notable Malesian element.

THE ANTARCTIC KINGDOM

This kingdom includes the southern tip of South America, extending some distance north along the Chilean coast; New Zealand; and the Antarctic and subantarctic islands. Antarctic and Paleotropical flora occur in an interesting and interdigitating pattern in South Island of New Zealand, Tasmania, and the Australian Alps. According to Good, about 50 genera are common in this kingdom.

Southern Chile, Patagonia, and New Zealand comprise the Subantarctic region. It has a distinctive forest flora, of which *Nothofagus* (southern beech) is perhaps the most characteristic element.

The Antarctic region includes the Antarctic islands and areas on the margin of the continent. The flora of this region is exceedingly impoverished. In general, flowering plants do not survive the harsh climate well, and mosses and other cryptogams form the main element. Traces of true Antarctic flora can be found at higher altitudes in New Zealand and southern Australia, especially Tasmania.

THE FAUNAL REALMS

Although the earliest study of the geographic distribution of animals was that of Sclater in 1858, it was Wallace who set

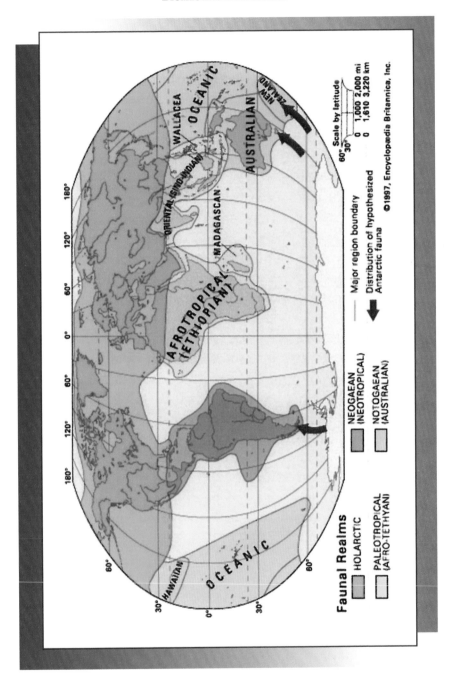

A map delineating Earth's faunal realms. Copyright Encyclopaedia Britannica; rendering for this edition by Rosen Educational Services.

the parameters to determine the zoogeographic regions, or realms, in his classic book, *The Geographical Distribution of Animals* (1876). Wallace recognized three realms: Megagaea or Arcotogaea, which includes Africa, Eurasia, and North America; Notogaea, including Australia, Oceania, and New Zealand; and Neogaea, including Central and South America. His divisions, although modified, form the basis of the realms recognized today.

Although different species have different dispersal abilities, even bird and insect distributions can be accounted for by traditional zoogeographic boundaries. In general, the distribution of terrestrial mammals, fresh-water fish, and invertebrates seem to correspond well and provide the best evidence of zoogeographic divisions.

The zones where faunas mix have in many cases been well studied. Some classifications arbitrarily include them in one region (or realm), and some omit them from any formal assignment and relegate them to a Subtraction-Transition zone. An example of such a zone is Wallacea, which includes the Philippines, Celebes, the Moluccas, and the Lesser Sundas. Located between the Paleotropical and Australian realms, Wallacea contains a mixture of both regions. The fauna is impoverished and unbalanced, but the area does have a high endemicity.

The following divisions are based on and modified to a great degree from the work of P.J. Darlington.

THE HOLARCTIC REALM

The Holarctic is usually divided on the basis of terrestrial organisms into two regions: Nearctic (North America) and Palearctic (Eurasia and North Africa). Unlike the North American phytogeographic region, the Nearctic zoogeographic region extends south to include all of Florida and Baja California. Some intriguing disjunct distributions are found in the Holarctic: some taxa are

WALLACE'S LINE

Wallace's Line is the name of the boundary between the Oriental and Australian faunal regions, proposed by the 19th-century British naturalist Alfred Russel Wallace. The line extends from the Indian Ocean through the Lombok Strait (between the islands of Bali and Lombok), northward through the Makassar Strait (between Borneo and Celebes), and eastward, south of Mindanao, into the Philippine Sea. Although many zoogeographers no longer consider Wallace's Line a regional boundary, it does represent an abrupt limit of distribution for many major animal groups. Many fish, bird, and mammal groups are abundantly represented on one side of Wallace's Line but poorly or not at all on the other side.

shared between Europe and eastern North America, some between Europe and eastern Asia, and others between western North America and eastern Asia. These distributions are perhaps explicable on the basis of the movement, in the recent past, of climatic zones.

Specialists on freshwater fish and invertebrates prefer to divide the Holarctic more finely. Petru Banarescu recognizes the following regions: Euro-Mediterranean; Siberian, Baikal, and Western Mongolian; Eastern, Western, and Arctic North American; and Central Mexican.

Among the families characteristic of this realm are mammals such as Talpidae (moles), Castoridae (beavers), Ochotonidae (pikas); amphibians such as three families of salamanders, Salamandridae, Cryptobranchidae, and Proteidae; and invertebrates such as the freshwater crayfish family Astacidae.

THE PALEOTROPICAL REALM

The Paleotropical, or Afro-Tethyan, realm is clearly divided into two regions, which are sometimes regarded as separate realms: the Afrotropical, which includes continental Africa south of the Sahara and southwestern Arabia, and the Oriental, which includes tropical southern and southeastern Asia, including associated continental islands. Two other regions, Madagascar and Wallacea, are commonly separated from the two main ones.

Being in continuous geographic contact, the Paleotropical and the Holarctic realms merge into one another. Nevertheless, each has many distinct elements, in part but not entirely because of their different climates. The mammalian orders Pholidota (pangolins) and Proboscidea (elephants) are endemic to the Paleotropical region. Mammalian families that are confined to and extend across the realm include the Cercopithecidae (Old World monkeys), Lorisidae (lorises, bush babies, angwantibo, and potto), Hystricidae (Old World porcupines), Viverridae (civets and mongooses), Rhinocerotidae (rhinoceroses), and Tragulidae (chevrotains). Endemic avian families include Bucerotidae (hornbills) and Pittidae (pittas); and endemic reptilian families, Chamaeleontidae (Old World chameleons).

The line between the Afrotropical, or Ethiopian, region and the Holarctic is generally drawn somewhere across the Sahara desert. A radical reanalysis of mammal distributions by Charles H. Smith, however, has concluded that the Mediterranean region, including both its southern and northern shores, is actually much more Paleotropical than Holarctic in aspect. Strictly speaking, the term Afro-Tethyan (in reference to the Tethys Sea, the waterway separating Laurasia from Gondwana during the Mesozoic Era) would apply to this expanded concept.

In striking contrast to the plant life in the southern tip of Africa, which makes up the South African, or Capensic, kingdom, the fauna of the Cape region cannot be distinguished from that of the surrounding regions. Presumably any unique faunal Capensic element that may have existed at one time has merged with the tropical element. African mainland endemic taxa include the mammalian orders Hyracoidea (hyraxes), Tubulidentata (aardvarks), and Macroscelidea (elephant shrews); the mammalian families Chrysochloridae (golden moles), Pedetidae (springhares), Thryonomyidae (cane rats), and Giraffidae (giraffes and okapi); the bird families Struthionidae (ostriches), Balaenicipitidae (shoebills), and Sagittaridae (secretary birds); the frog subfamily Phrynomerinae; the freshwater fish subclass Palaeopterygii (bichirs), and families Mormyridae (snoutfish) and Malapteruridae (electric catfish); and the snail family Aillyidae.

Madagascar is so different from the continent of Africa that it is generally given equal status as a separate region. Mammalian families shared with the African mainland (Paleotropical realm) include Tenrecidae (tenrecs and otter shrews) and Hippopotamidae (hippopotamuses, which have recently become extinct in Madagascar). Madagascar also shares some groups with the Neotropical realm, notably iguanas and boas, which the rest of the Paleotropical realm presumably lost during the Paleogene and Neogene periods (65.5 million to 2.6 million years ago). Madagascan endemics include, among mammals, several families of lemurs. Distinctive subgroups of tenrec insectivores, carnivores, and murid rodents also are endemic, as are the avian family Aepyornithidae (the recently extinct elephant birds) and other subfamilies and families of birds. Familiar African mainland animals, such as monkeys, antelopes, elephants, rhinoceroses, and big cats, are absent.

Seychelles and the Mascarene Islands have distant Madagascan affinities and are generally included in the Madagascan region.

Endemic families in the Oriental, or Sino-Indian, region include, among mammals, the Tupaiidae (tree shrews), Tarsiidae (tarsiers), and Hylobatidae (gibbons); among reptiles, the Lanthanotidae (earless monitor

Hippopotamuses still roam the African continent but are now extinct on the nearby island of Madagascar, which is considered its own unique biogeographic region. www.istockphoto.com / Nico Smit

lizards) and Gavialidae (the crocodile-like gharials); and a few bird and invertebrate families.

The three-way boundary between the Oriental and Afrotropical regions and the Holarctic realm is difficult to define; essentially the entire area of Southwest Asia is transitional. Certain areas within this span, however, are more clear-cut: the Negev and the Red Sea coast of Arabia are predominantly Afrotropical, while Syria, Iraq, Iran, and Afghanistan show decreasing Afrotropical affinities as well as links to the Holarctic. A distinctive desert fauna, often referred to as Saharo-Sindian, unites the entire region and has been allocated by different authorities to any one of the three regions.

Mammalian specialists such as G.B. Corbet place the approximate boundary between the Oriental region and the Holarctic in central China; however, Banarescu extends what he calls the Sino-Indian region north to include the Tien Shan mountain system, Tibet, and the Huang Ho, based on evidence of freshwater fish and invertebrates.

Much debate has centred around the dividing line between the Oriental region and the Australian (Notogaean) realm. Wallace considered the edge of the continental shelf of Asia (the Sunda Shelf) to form the border of this region, and Wallace's Line is the demarcation, east of Borneo, Bali, and the Philippines, of the "typical" Oriental fauna. The basis for this division is the striking difference between faunas to the east and west of the line. Subsequent debate has continued for generations about the position of this boundary. The northern part of the line was altered by T.H. Huxley to fall to the west of the Philippines (excluding Palawan). Huxley's line is considered a more appropriate delineation by some zoogeographers (e.g., G.G. Simpson) because the Philippines has a highly idiosyncratic fauna.

The famous zoogeographic transition zone called Wallacea is located in central Indonesia. This zone, usually included in the Paleotropical realm, is bounded to the west by Huxley's Line (or a variation thereof) and to the east by Lydekker's Line, which runs along the border of Australia's continental shelf (the Sahul Shelf); it includes a mixture of Oriental and Australian fauna. Weber's Line, which runs west of the Moluccas, represents the area where the two types of fauna are equally mixed. No comparable floral division is apparent. Celebes and the Philippines excepting Palawan, which is Oriental, contain somewhat unbalanced faunas. Most of these faunas are generically distinct from their Oriental relatives, although some, such as those of Celebes, include a few Australian elements. Flores, in the Lesser Sundas, has, or had, a very few but distinctive genera, as did Timor. In the Moluccas the faunal affinities are clearly with New Guinea.

The Notogaean, or Australian, realm begins east of Lydekker's Line and extends out into the Pacific Ocean. It consists of four regions: Australian, Oceanic, New Zealand, and Hawaiian. The faunas of many of the Pacific Islands, however, have as much in common with the Paleotropical fauna as with the Australian fauna proper. Endemic to the region are the monotremes (egg-laying mammals such as the platypus [Ornithorhynchus anatinus]), four of the six orders of marsupials, many families of birds and fish, and some invertebrates. Gondwanan affinities include ratites (flightless birds), lungfish, the reptilian families Chelydae (snake-necked turtles) and the extinct Meiolaniidae (horned tortoises), the frog families Hylidae (tree frogs) and Leptodactylidae, and several invertebrate families.

The Australian region proper includes Australia, New Guinea, and the Solomon Islands. Bird orders such as Rheiformes (rheas) and Casuariiformes (cassowaries) and families such as Menuridae (lyrebirds) and Paradisaeidae (birds-of-paradise) are endemic to the region, which is the only part of the Notogaean realm that contains any mammals, except bats. The inclusion of New Guinea in this region is interesting; the New Guinean fauna comprises the rainforest aspect of the Australian fauna. The disparity in the biological affinities of this large island exemplifies perhaps one of the most striking differences between phytogeography and zoogeography. (As mentioned above, the flora of New Guinea is classified as Paleotropical, but the fauna is not included in the comparable faunal realm.)

The Oceanic region is poorly defined. It contains some localized endemics, notably the bird family Rhynochetidae (kagu) in New Caledonia. Much of the fauna, especially birds, is of demonstrable Australian affinity.

The New Zealand region includes all of New Zealand, excluding aspects of the fauna of the southwest, which shows an Antarctic element. Flightless birds inhabit both New Zealand and Australia, although the order Dinornithiformes (kiwis and moas) is endemic to New Zealand. Other endemic taxa include the snail family Athoracophoridae; New Zealand's only mammals, the bat family Mystacinidae; Xenicidae (New Zealand wrens); Leiopelmatidae (a primitive family of frogs); and Sphenodontidae (tuatara, a primitive reptile family).

The Hawaiian region consists entirely of Hawaii and its outlying islands. The region boasts a few endemic invertebrate families and one avian family, Drepanididae (Hawaiian honeycreepers).

THE NEOGAEAN REALM

The Neogaean, or Neotropical, realm extends south from the tropical lowlands of Mexico through Central America into South America as far as the temperate and subantarctic zones and includes the West Indies. Among endemic mammal groups, the Didelphimorphia (an order of marsupials) and several distinctive placental orders, such as the Edentata (and several extinct orders), have been present since the Paleocene (65.5 million to 55.8 million years ago). By the Oligocene (33.9 million to 23 million years ago) the platyrrhines (New World monkeys) and a group of rodents (the Caviomorpha) had entered South America by means that are still not understood. Among birds, two entire orders—the flightless Rheiformes (rheas) and Tinamiformes (tinamous)—and 30 families are endemic. Some fish and invertebrate taxa also are endemic. Many of these endemic taxa are believed to date from Gondwanan times (the Early Cretaceous), when the southern continents formed a single landmass. Evidence for this view is provided by the presence in Africa and Australia of their nearest relatives—e.g., the flightless birds, lungfish, bony fish families such as Cichlidae, and many invertebrates (notably the primitive Onychophora, known as velvet worms).

In the West Indies, which are an impoverished region within Neogaea, distinctive mammals include two endemic insectivore families, Solenodontidae (solenodon, almiqui) and the recently extinct Nesophontidae. The Galapagos Islands have an impoverished fauna ultimately derived from South America.

The Antarctic Realm

The Antarctic, or Archinotic, realm encompasses the Antarctic continent, subantarctic islands, and elements of southwestern New Zealand. The existence of the realm—or rather of its ghost, because nowhere today does it exist in an umixed state—is justified by the common occurrence in New Zealand and South America of such groups as the Eustheniidae (a family of stoneflies), the crustacean order Stygocaridacea, and certain freshwater snails. It is plausible that the marsupial family Microbiotheriidae, which is confined to Chile and is more closely related to the Australian marsupials than to other South American ones, is a relic of an Antarctic connection.

ECOSYSTEMS

An ecosystem is the complex of living organisms, their physical environment, and all their interrelationships in a particular unit of space. It can be categorized into its abiotic (that is, nonliving) constituents, including minerals, climate, soil, water, sunlight, and all other nonliving elements, and its biotic constituents, consisting of all its living members. Linking these constituents together are two major forces: the flow of energy through the ecosystem, and the cycling of nutrients within the ecosystem.

The fundamental source of energy in almost all ecosystems is radiant energy from the sun. The energy of sunlight is used by the ecosystem's autotrophic, or self-sustaining, organisms. Consisting largely of green vegetation, these organisms are capable of photosynthesis—i.e., they can use the energy of sunlight to convert carbon dioxide and water into simple, energy-rich carbohydrates. The autotrophs use the energy stored within the simple carbohydrates to produce the more complex organic compounds, such as proteins, lipids, and starches, that maintain the organisms' life processes. The autotrophic segment of the ecosystem is commonly referred to as the producer level.

Organic matter generated by autotrophs directly or indirectly sustains heterotrophic organisms. Heterotrophs are the consumers of the ecosystem; they cannot make their own food. They use, rearrange, and ultimately decompose the complex organic materials built up by the autotrophs. All animals and fungi are heterotrophs, as are most bacteria and many other microorganisms.

Together, the autotrophs and heterotrophs form various trophic (feeding) levels in the ecosystem. The producer level is composed of those organisms that make their own food. The primary-consumer level is composed of those organisms that feed on producers, and the secondary-consumer level is composed of those organisms that feed on primary consumers, and so on. The movement of organic matter and energy from the producer level through various consumer levels makes up a food chain. For example, a typical food chain in a grassland might be grass (producer) → mouse (primary consumer) → snake (secondary consumer) → hawk (tertiary consumer).

Actually, in many cases the food chains of the ecosystem overlap and interconnect, forming what ecologists call a food web. The final link in all food chains is made up of decomposers, those heterotrophs that break down dead organisms and organic wastes. A food chain in which the primary consumer feeds on living plants is called a grazing pathway; that in which the primary consumer feeds on dead plant matter is known as a detritus pathway. Both pathways are important in accounting for the energy budget of the ecosystem.

BIOLOGICAL COMMUNITIES

A biological community is an interacting group of various species in a common location. For example, a forest of trees and undergrowth plants, inhabited by animals and rooted in soil containing bacteria and fungi, constitutes a biological community.

Among the factors that determine the overall structure of a community are the number of species (diversity) within it, the number of each species (abundance) found within it, the interactions among the species, and the ability of the community to return to normal after a disruptive influence such as fire or drought. The change of biological communities over time is known as succession, or ecological succession.

The various species in a community each occupy their own ecological niche. The niche of a species includes all of its interactions with other members of the community, including competition, predation, parasitism, and mutualism. The organisms within a community can be positioned along food chains by showing which eats which, and these positions are known as trophic levels. The first level includes the producers—the photosynthetic plants—which convert the Sun's radiant energy into nutrients available to other organisms in the community.

ECOTONES

A transition area of vegetation between two different plant communities, such as forest and grassland, is known as an ecotone. It has some of the characteristics of each bordering community and often contains species not found in the overlapping communities. An ecotone may exist along a broad belt or in a small pocket, such as a forest clearing, where two local communities blend together. The influence of the two bordering communities on each other is known as the edge effect. An ecotonal area often has a higher density of organisms of one species and a greater number of species than are found in either flanking community. Some organisms need a transitional area for activities such as courtship, nesting, or foraging for food.

These plants are eaten by herbivores (plant-eaters, or primary consumers), the second trophic level. Herbivores are, in turn, eaten by carnivores (flesh-eaters), which are frequently eaten by larger carnivores (secondary and tertiary consumers, respectively). The food chain ends when the last link dies and is attacked by various bacteria and fungi, the decomposers that break down dead organic matter and thereby release essential nutrients back into the environment.

CHAPTER 4
TERRESTRIAL ECOSYSTEM CASE STUDIES

Earth has tremendous diversity in both life-forms and physical features. Both contribute to the formation and development of ecosystems. The structure of the ecosystem determines and is at some level determined by the biological players. Feeding and decomposition pathways and the effects of competition and other interactions between and within species affect nutrient cycling and energy flow through ecosystems. Although multitudes of ecosystems exist on Earth, the case studies described below provide a sampling of how biological, chemical, and geological forces interact to produce unique settings for living things.

THE MOUNTAIN ECOSYSTEM

Mountain ecosystems are made up of living organisms and the nonliving environments they inhabit in highland areas. Mountain lands provide a scattered but diverse array of habitats in which a large range of plants and animals can be found. At higher altitudes harsh environmental conditions generally prevail, and a treeless alpine vegetation, upon which the present account is focused, is supported. Lower slopes commonly are covered by montane forests. At even lower levels mountain lands grade into other types of landform and vegetation—e.g., tropical or temperate forest, savanna, scrubland, desert, or tundra.

The largest and highest area of mountain lands occurs in the Himalaya-Tibet region; the longest nearly continuous mountain range is that along the west coast of the Americas from Alaska in the north to Chile in the south. Other particularly significant areas of mountain lands include those in Europe (Alps, Pyrenees), Asia (Caucasus, Urals), New Guinea, New Zealand, and East Africa.

THE ORIGIN OF MOUNTAIN ECOSYSTEMS

Viewed against a geologic time frame, the processes of mountain uplift and erosion occur relatively quickly, and high mountain ranges therefore are somewhat transient features. Many mountains are isolated from other regions of similar environmental conditions, their summit regions resembling recently formed islands of cool climate settled amid large areas of different, warmer climates. Because of this isolation, mountaintops harbour a distinct biota of youthful assemblages of plants and animals adapted to cold temperatures. At lower elevations, however, some mountains are able to provide refuges for more ancient biota displaced by environmental changes. Also, mountainous vegetation usually has been affected less by human activities than the surrounding areas and so may harbour plants and animals that have been driven out by anthropogenic disturbances that have occurred elsewhere.

During the glacial intervals of the past two million years—the Ice Ages of the Northern Hemisphere—habitats suitable to cold-adapted biota covered much larger areas than they do today, and considerable migration of cold-adapted plants and animals occurred. Arctic biota spread south across large areas beyond the greatly expanded ice sheets that covered much of northern North America, Europe, and Asia. When climatic conditions ameliorated, these organisms retreated both northward toward Arctic latitudes and uphill into areas of mountainous terrain. This history explains, for example, the close similarities between the fauna and flora of high mountains such as the European Alps and the Arctic far to their north.

In the tropics, however, little opportunity for similar overland movement of cold-adapted biota was possible because vast forestland in the tropical lowlands formed a barrier to migration. The organisms therefore have been isolated more completely from those of other cold environments. Despite this situation, colonization of tropical high mountains has occurred. Birds are particularly mobile, and some of temperate affinity found their way to equatorial peaks; for example, in the mountains of New Guinea are found pipits and thrushes that have no near relatives in the adjacent tropical lowlands. Migrating birds may have been the vectors for the seeds of cold-adapted plants growing in the same places, which also lack tropical lowland relatives.

Populations of mountain species are commonly both small—although fluctuating—and isolated and often have evolved over a relatively short period of time. It is therefore not unusual to encounter related but distinct species on separate mountain peaks. This recent and rapid production of new species contributes significantly to the biodiversity and biological importance of mountain lands.

MOUNTAIN ENVIRONMENTS

Mountain environments have different climates from the surrounding lowlands, and hence the vegetation differs as well. The differences in climate result from two principal causes: altitude and relief. Altitude affects climate because atmospheric temperature drops with increasing altitude by about 0.5 to 0.6 °C (0.9 to 1.1 °F) per 100 metres (328 feet). The relief of mountains affects climate because they stand in the path of wind systems and force air to rise over them. As the air rises it cools, leading to higher precipitation on windward mountain slopes (orographic

BIODIVERSITY

Biodiversity, which is also called biological diversity, is the variety of life found in a place on Earth or, often, the total variety of life on Earth. A common measure of this variety, called species richness, is the count of species in an area. Colombia and Kenya, for example, each have more than 1,000 breeding species of birds, whereas the forests of Great Britain and of eastern North America are home to fewer than 200. A coral reef off northern Australia may have 500 species of fish, while the rocky shoreline of Japan may be home to only 100 species. Such numbers capture some of the differences between places—the tropics, for example, have more biodiversity than temperate regions—but raw species count is not the only measure of diversity. Furthermore, biodiversity encompasses the genetic variety within each species and the variety of ecosystems that species create.

A second way to weight species biodiversity is to recognize the unique biodiversity of those environments that contain few species but unusual ones. Dramatic examples come from extreme environments such as the summits of active Antarctic volcanoes (e.g., Mt. Erebus and Mt. Melbourne in the Ross Sea region), hot springs (e.g., Yellowstone National Park in the western United States), or deep-sea hydrothermal vents. The numbers of species found in these places may be smaller than almost anywhere else, yet the species are quite distinctive.

In addition to diversity among species, the concept of biodiversity includes the genetic diversity within species. One example is the human species, for humans differ in a wide variety of characteristics that are partly or wholly genetically determined, including height, weight, skin and eye colour, behavioral traits, and resistance to various diseases.

The catalog of Earth's biodiversity is incomplete. About 1.5 million species have scientific names. Estimates of the total number of living species cluster around 10 million, which means that most species have not been discovered and described. (These estimates omit bacteria because of the practical problems in defining bacterial species.) Of the 1.5 million species now described, perhaps two-thirds are known from only one location and many from examining only one individual or a limited number of individuals, so knowledge of the genetic variation within species is even more constrained. From just a few well-studied species, it is clear that genetic variability can be substantial and that it differs in extent between species.

precipitation); as it descends leeward slopes it becomes warmer and relative humidity falls, reducing the likelihood of precipitation and creating areas of drier climate (rain shadows).

While these general principles apply to all mountains, particular mountain climates vary. For instance, mountains in desert regions receive little rain because the air is almost always too dry to permit precipitation under any conditions—e.g., the Ahaggar Mountains in southern Algeria in the middle of the Sahara. Latitude also can affect mountain climates. On mountains in equatorial regions winter and summer are nonexistent, although temperatures at high altitude are low. Above about 3,500 metres (about 11,500 feet) frost may form any night of the year, but in the middle of every day temperatures warm substantially beneath the nearly vertical tropical sun, thus producing a local climate of "winter every night and spring every day." For example, at an altitude of 4,760 metres (about 15,600 feet) in Peru, temperatures range from an average minimum of about -2 °C (28 °F) to average maximum values of 5 to 8 °C (41 to 46 °F) in every month of the year.

By contrast, mountains at temperate latitudes have strongly marked seasons. Above the tree line during the summer season, temperatures high enough for plant growth occur for only about 100 days, but this period may be virtually frost-free even at night. During the long winter, however, temperatures may remain below freezing day and night. Snow accumulation and the phenomena this type of precipitation may cause, such as avalanching, are important ecological factors in temperate but not tropical mountain regions.

Microclimate variations are also important in mountain regions, with different aspects of steep slopes exhibiting contrasting conditions due to variations in precipitation and solar energy receipt. In temperate regions mountain slopes facing the Equator—southward in the Northern Hemisphere and northward in the Southern Hemisphere—are significantly warmer than opposite slopes. This can directly and indirectly influence the vegetation; the length of time snow remains on the ground into spring affects when vegetation will emerge, and this in turn affects the land's utility for grazing. Even in the tropics, aspect-related climate and vegetation contrasts occur, in spite of the midday vertical position of the sun. In New Guinea, for example, slopes facing east are warmer and drier and support certain plants at higher altitudes than slopes facing west, because the prevailing pattern of clear, sunny mornings and cloudy afternoons affects the amount of solar energy received by these contrasting aspects.

Mountain soils are usually shallow at higher altitudes, partly because the soil has been scraped off by the ice caps that formed on most high mountains throughout the world during the last glacial interval that ended about 10,000 years ago. Soils are generally poor in nutrients important to plants, especially nitrogen. Rapid erosion of loose materials is also common and is exacerbated by frost heaving, steep slopes, and, in temperate regions, substantial runoff of meltwater in spring. Soil is virtually absent on rocky peaks and ridges. However, because of the cool, wet climate, many mountain areas accumulate peat, which creates local deep, wet, acidic soils. In volcanic regions tephra (erupted ash) may also contribute to soil depth and fertility.

Considering the wide geographic extent of mountains and their resultant geologic and climatic variability, it is remarkable that they exhibit such a clear overall pattern in vegetation. The major structural feature of vegetation on mountains in all regions—except in very dry or very cold places—is tree line. (This characteristic is sometimes called timberline or forest limit, although strictly speaking the former term refers to the uppermost reaches that commercial-size timber trees attain and the latter term refers to a closed forest.) Above a critical level, which may vary between slopes on the same mountain and which is much higher on mountains at lower latitude, the climate becomes too harsh to permit tree growth; beyond that level grows alpine vegetation, dominated by herbaceous plants, such as grasses and forbs, or by low shrubs.

In general, the altitude at which the tree line occurs is determined by that at which the mean temperature in the warmest month approximates 10 °C (50 °F), provided moisture is not a limiting factor. This is not precisely the

A distinguishing pattern of vegetation growth in mountainous ecosystems is the tree line, where trees abruptly stop growing because the climate is too harsh to support even hearty cold-weather conifers. Photo 24/Brand X Pictures/ Getty Images

case under all circumstances, however; for example, in some tropical regions that have a yearlong growing season, forests can grow in conditions slightly cooler than this. Nevertheless, the value holds true in most regions, especially in the temperate zones. It reflects a fundamental requirement for a sufficient level of photosynthesis to occur to support the growth of tree trunks.

A relatively narrow belt of intermediate or mixed vegetation—the subalpine—usually exists between the forests below and the alpine vegetation above. In the subalpine of temperate mountains, stunted, usually infertile individuals of various tree species survive, despite blasts of windblown snow, frost damage, and desiccation. These deformed shrub-size trees are called krummholz.

Although the overall pattern in which forest gives way to alpine vegetation is common to mountains at all latitudes, the factors responsible for it are not the same in all places. In temperate-zone mountains, the brevity of the growing season is of paramount importance because tree shoot tissues that have had insufficient time to harden before growth ceases and winter conditions begin may die when frozen. Other factors that damage or kill shoots or entire trees in winter in this region at temperate latitudes include the abrasion of buds by windblown snow crystals, desiccation of shoots just above the snowpack where they are exposed to direct and snow-reflected solar radiation—especially late in winter as the sun angle rises—and infection of shoots beneath the snow by snow fungus. Freezing injury to roots may also occur if the insulating layer of snow is blown from the ground surface.

In the tropics, these phenomena are not experienced. Snowfall is not restricted to a single winter season, and when it occurs it usually melts quickly. Snow therefore does not accumulate as a thick, continuous cover except at altitudes above the upper limit of most plant life. For example, in Venezuela the tree line lies below 4,000 metres (about 13,100 feet), even where there has been no human disturbance, but virtually permanent snowpatches are not encountered until about 5,000 metres (about 16,400 feet), where no vascular plants survive. Tree line in tropical regions is a consequence of low maximum temperatures throughout the year. However, the microclimate near the ground is warmer, allowing prostrate shrubs to grow at altitudes well above the highest trees.

THE FLORA OF MOUNTAIN ECOSYSTEMS

Mountains in north temperate regions, such as those of North America, Europe, and northern Asia, generally have conifer-dominated forest on their lower slopes that gives way to alpine vegetation above. Typical conifers in these mountain regions are pines (*Pinus*), firs (*Abies*), spruces (*Picea*), and the deciduous larches (*Larix*). Some areas have broad-leaved deciduous trees, and a variety of smaller plants are found beneath the trees, especially in moister spots. For example, mountains in the northern half of Japan that are higher than 1,400 to 1,500 metres (about 4,600 to 4,900 feet) have a subarctic coniferous forest belt, the dominant trees all being conifers in the genera *Abies*, *Picea*, and *Larix*. Heathers, poppies, and the large carrot relative *Oplopanax* are a few of the other plants that grow in these forests. In some areas moorland vegetation is found, dominated by the moss *Sphagnum*. Birch (*Betula*) fringes the forest at its upper limit and occupies areas with a history of burning. In the Pacific Northwest of North America *Pinus*, *Picea*, and *Abies* usually dominate tree line forests. Aspens (*Populus tremuloides*) occur in places, especially those areas with a history of disturbance. Alders (*Alnus*) are found in avalanche tracks, and willows (*Salix*) are important species in wet places. Lupins (*Lupinus*), pasqueflowers (*Anemone*), and a large variety of daisies and low shrubs in the heather family are examples of the rich flora of smaller plants that grow beneath the trees and in meadows near the tree line.

Tree line forests in south temperate mountain regions also are dominated by only one or very few different types of tree at any site; the trees involved are usually broad-leaved rather than coniferous. For instance, most Australian mountains have tree line forests dominated by *Eucalyptus*, although a long history of widespread burning may be responsible to some extent for the prominence of this fire-tolerant tree. In New Zealand, Argentina, and Chile the tree line commonly consists of *Nothofagus* species.

In the tropics, by contrast, species-diverse forests that can be described as stunted evergreen rainforests typically grow as far as the uppermost limits of tree growth. This is the case in New Guinea, Southeast Asia, and East Africa; however, in parts of the tropical Andes, single species of *Polylepis* (of the rose family) often grow at altitudes above all other trees, especially on screes (rock debris that has accumulated at the base of a cliff).

Above the tree line, alpine vegetation comprises a variety of different subtypes including grasslands, mires, low heathlands, and crevice-occupying vegetation. For example, treeless alpine vegetation is found on mountains above 2,500 metres (8,200 feet) in central Japan, grading down to 1,400 metres (4,600 feet) in northern Hokkaido. Japanese stone pine (*Pinus pumila*), heathers, and grasses are particularly prominent. Like most other plants in this alpine vegetation, these plants have near relatives in the alpine areas of other mountainous, north temperate regions. The prostrate shrubs of the stone pine form

Vegetation profile of tropical mountain lands. Encyclopædia Britannica, Inc.

dense, low thickets about one metre tall on ridges; they are mixed with deciduous shrubs of alder and service tree (*Sorbus*) in moister places. Other alpine communities occupy wet sites, where tall grassy meadows or bog communities often boast abundant tiny primroses (*Primula nipponica*). Stunted dwarf shrubs, especially members of the heather family and their relatives *Arcterica*, *Vaccinium*, *Diapensia*, and *Empetrum* occur where winter snow is blown from exposed surfaces.

Conversely, in places where snow accumulates as deep drifts in sheltered spots and where it remains until late spring or summer, snowbed communities occur that are dominated by the heather *Phyllodoce* or by sedges (species of *Carex*), with many other small plants also present. Alpine deserts are also widespread in the high mountains of Japan, in places with marked soil instability associated with the effects of recent volcanic activity. While the plants surviving in such places are varied, some, like the violet *Viola crassa*, are typical of these harsh habitats.

Remarkably, the flora in the diverse array of alpine vegetation subtypes, such as in the above example, typically consists of a similar number of different plant species—about 200—in many regions both temperate and tropical. Furthermore, despite wide ecological and geographic contrasts, many of the same types of plant are found in most alpine regions. They are usually represented by different though related species in each region and on each mountain within regions. Gentians (*Gentiana*), plantains (*Plantago*), buttercups (*Ranunculus*), and members of the heather, grass, and sedge families are widespread examples.

However, some regional peculiarities exist both in alpine flora and in vegetation structure. One striking example concerns the large stem rosette plants found on several high tropical, but not temperate, mountains. These are giant herbs that reach three metres (about 10 feet) in height or beyond; they have persistent dead leaf bases that insulate the water-containing tissues of the stem from freezing conditions that can occur virtually every night in their very high (up to 4,300 metres [about 14,100 feet]), dry environments. Similar but unrelated stem rosette plants are found in the northern Andes (*Espeletia* and *Puya*) and on mountains in East Africa (*Dendrosenecio* and *Lobelia*), with other examples in Hawaii, Java, and the Himalayas. This emergence of the same characteristic among different species that are under the same environmental pressures on different continents is an example of convergent evolution.

THE FAUNA OF MOUNTAIN ECOSYSTEMS

Mountain fauna is less distinctive than the flora of the same places and usually reflects the regional fauna. For example, the large mammals of North American mountain lands include deer, bears, wolves, and several large cats, all of which inhabit, or did before human invasion, the surrounding areas beyond the mountains. Some birds are tied to mountain habitats, such as the condors of the high ranges of California and the Andes. On certain mountains, flightless insects such as grasshoppers are a feature of interest, a phenomenon that is particularly pronounced on East African peaks such as Kilimanjaro.

As a result of their range of diverse topographic and climatic environments, and because evolution of cold-adapted biota has often proceeded independently on separate mountains in the same area, mountain regions are often noted as being centres of high biodiversity. The Caucasus Mountains in Asia provide one well-known example, while, in the tropics, the mountains of New Guinea contribute greatly to an enormous diversity of organisms, including some 20,000 plant species that represent 10 percent of the world's flora.

THE DEVELOPMENT AND STRUCTURE OF POPULATIONS AND COMMUNITIES IN MOUNTAIN ECOSYSTEMS

Population and community processes in temperate mountain regions, as in the rather similar Arctic environments, are influenced by the highly seasonal climate. As the winter snowpack melts, plants undergo a surge of growth and flowering, particularly in the alpine zone where the entire growing season is completed within about three months. Substantial food reserves in subterranean organs are used to generate mature, fertile shoots very rapidly, with growth in some cases beginning under the snow before melt is complete. Because almost the entire alpine flora blooms within the same period of only a few weeks and because alpine plants tend to have relatively large flowers, the floral display to be seen in temperate mountains in summer is often spectacular. In tropical mountains there is no such period of spectacular development that alternates with a longer season of enforced dormancy, and plants grow throughout the year unless their development is stopped by the onset of a dry season.

Animal activity similarly varies seasonally between regions. In temperate mountains there is a long period during which most birds and larger mammals migrate to lower altitudes. Some remaining mammals, such as the gophers of North American mountains, take advantage of the insulated environment beneath the snow where they make burrows and feed on subterranean plant organs.

In tropical mountains seasonal changes are much less pronounced, and this is reflected in animal reproduction. For example, birds on high mountains in New Guinea may breed throughout the year. However, because there is no seasonal flush of plant and insect growth creating a temporarily abundant source of food, they lay few eggs. Clutches of only one or two are normal there, by contrast with the five to eight eggs typically laid by many temperate mountain birds during their brief breeding season.

Biological Productivity in Mountain Ecosystems

As stressful habitats for plants, mountain lands are not very productive environments. The biomass (dry weight of organic matter in an area) of the alpine vegetation on high temperate mountains, however, may be greater than it first appears because more than 10 times the amount of visible, aboveground biomass is present below the ground in the form of roots, rhizomes, tubers, and bulbs. By contrast, plants of the tropical alpine flora do not need to store food below ground, and less than half of the total biomass is located there.

Agricultural exploitation of mountain lands, therefore, is not very productive and generally is not intensive, being mainly confined to light or seasonal grazing by cattle, goats, and sheep. Where it occurs at moderate intensity, grazing can be very destructive to alpine vegetation, which cannot easily cope with disturbance in its already environmentally stressful state. Similarly, the physical disturbance associated with other human uses of high mountains, such as skiing and other forms of recreation, can be permanently damaging. Another concern is that atmospheric pollutants tend to become concentrated in snowfall. In temperate regions a pulse of polluting substances enters the alpine system with the annual snowmelt, bringing possibly detrimental consequences in this low-nutrient environment.

THE POLAR ECOSYSTEM

Polar ecosystems are made up of the living and nonliving parts of environments in cold regions, such as in polar barrens and tundra. Polar barrens and tundra are found at high latitudes on land surfaces not covered by perpetual ice and snow. These areas lying beyond the tree line comprise more than 10 percent of the Earth's land surface. Most are in the Arctic and subarctic, as little land area in the Antarctic is ever free of snow and ice. The Arctic can be divided into the Low Arctic and High Arctic, according to various environmental and biological characteristics. Tundras are most common in the Low Arctic region of North America and Eurasia, and polar barrens are dominant in the High Arctic.

Tundra and lakes during summer in the Yamal Peninsula of Siberia, Russia. Bryan and Cherry Alexander

The Russian term "tundra" is derived from the Finnish word *tunturi*, meaning treeless heights. Tundra is now used in a general sense to describe any cold-climate landscape having vegetation without trees, which includes both mountainous areas (alpine tundra) and areas in the Arctic, subarctic, and Antarctic. In a more restricted sense, tundra denotes a special type of vegetation association. Most regions—with the exception of rock outcrops, dry ridge tops, and river gravel bars—are fully vegetated, primarily by dwarf shrubs, lichens, and mosses. The tundra zones of the polar regions are distinct from the polar barrens, which are sparsely vegetated.

THE ORIGIN OF POLAR FLORA AND FAUNA

Compared with other biomes, the Arctic tundra biome is relatively young, having its origin in the Pleistocene (2.6

million to 11,700 years ago). Individual plant and animal species of the tundra, however, probably first appeared in the late Miocene (13.8 million to 5.3 million years ago) or early Pliocene (5.3 million to 3.6 million years ago). Coniferous forests were present on Ellesmere Island and in northern Greenland, the northernmost land areas, in the mid-Pliocene (3.6 million years ago). Most paleoecologists believe that tundra flora evolved from plants of the coniferous forests and alpine areas as continents drifted into higher and cooler latitudes during the Miocene (23 million to 5.3 million years ago).

In contrast, the continent of Antarctica has been isolated from other continental landmasses by broad expanses of ocean since early in the Paleogene Period, about 60 million to 40 million years ago. Prior to its separation it existed, along with Australia, South America, peninsular India, and Africa, as part of the landmass known as Gondwanaland. This long separation has impeded the establishment and development of land-based flora and fauna in the Antarctic. Other significant factors that have hampered terrestrial biotic evolution are the harsh climate, the ice cover that completely engulfed the continent during the Pleistocene glaciations, and the present limited number of ice-free land areas, which are restricted primarily to the coastal fringes and nunataks (mountain peaks surrounded by the ice cap). As a consequence, the terrestrial flora and fauna of Antarctica are few. The Antarctic Peninsula, which extends to 63° S, is the location of virtually all floral development of the Antarctic.

The Antarctic, however, encompasses not only the continent itself but also those islands lying within the Antarctic Convergence, where northward-flowing cold surface waters meet warmer subantarctic waters. Most

Antarctic islands, because of their position beyond the seasonal pack ice, are under much stronger maritime influence than comparable Arctic islands. The flora and fauna of these islands are poorly developed, largely because of their isolation from potential sources of terrestrial biota. South Georgia, the largest of these islands, lies 2,000 km (1,240 miles) east of Tierra del Fuego at 54° to 55° S and encompasses an area of 3,756 square km (1,450 square miles). Heavy precipitation and high mountains account for perennial snow cover at higher elevations and extensive glaciers.

Nevertheless, near sea level where soil formation has been possible, a unique Antarctic tundra vegetation has developed, dominated by tussock-forming grasses and mosses. Only 26 species of vascular plants are present, and there are no native land mammals, although reindeer introduced by Norwegian whalers in the early 1900s have established feral populations. Grazing by reindeer has altered plant communities by reduction or local elimination of the most preferred species.

POLAR ENVIRONMENTS

Characteristics of polar environments—the climate, substrates, elevation above sea level, slope, exposure, and proximity to other landmasses—determine the complex of plant and animal life present in the polar regions. It is the interplay of these factors during summer that determines whether temperatures are warm enough and moisture is sufficient to allow plants to grow. The High Arctic is distinguished from the Low Arctic based on ecological criteria, which include a shorter growing season, cooler summers, and a marked reduction in species of flora and fauna.

The southern limit of the tundra zone in the Northern Hemisphere may extend from 55° N at the southern tip of Hudson Bay in Canada along the northern Bering Sea coast of Alaska and the Russian Far East to above 70° N on the lower Mackenzie River of Canada, along the Khatanga River of central Siberia, and across northern Scandinavia. This limit generally coincides with the isoline of annual net solar radiation of 75 to 80 kilojoules per square cm, which closely parallels the 10 °C (50 °F) July isotherm. However, local variation in this boundary occurs in North America and Eurasia where influences of mountain ranges or warm ocean currents allow forests to penetrate northward to areas with as little as 67 kilojoules per square cm of radiation.

Daily summer temperatures may average only 2 to 5 °C (35 to 41 °F) in typical tundra and polar barrens, and the plant growth season is usually less than 100 days. Although summers are brief at high latitudes, the days of summer are long. At latitudes above the Arctic Circle (66°33' N) for at least a portion of the summer the Sun is above the horizon for 24 hours each day. This constant sunlight enables plants to optimize photosynthesis without the usual nighttime cost of respiration.

Total annual precipitation is low in the tundra and polar barrens, generally ranging between 100 and 1,000 mm (4 to 40 inches) per year. Precipitation is usually greatest near the coasts and at high altitudes. For example, in Greenland and Antarctica and at higher elevations on the Canadian Arctic Archipelago, permanent ice caps form. The low precipitation characteristic of tundra regions is comparable to that of deserts at lower latitudes. However, these regions are unlike true deserts in that the low temperatures in both winter and summer limit evaporation. Thus, a greater portion of the limited moisture from snowmelt and summer rains is available for plant growth. In addition, most tundra and polar barrens are underlain by soils that are permanently frozen (permafrost) except for a thin surface zone (active layer) that thaws each summer. The permafrost limits drainage and retains moisture for plant growth within the active layer. This can result in wetland formation, as occurs in level areas of the coastal plains of the Arctic, which contain extensive wetlands that are home to aquatic vegetation, invertebrate fauna, waterfowl, and shorebirds.

Circulation of air masses around the Earth transports industrial pollutants from temperate regions into the Arctic and Antarctic. Pollutants are becoming concentrated in these regions, and concern is growing over the possible consequences for life at high latitudes. Thinning of the ozone layer in the polar regions resulting from the industrial release of chlorofluorocarbons into the atmosphere may have long-term consequences for plant and animal life. Ultraviolet radiation, previously intercepted by the ozone layer, is detrimental to most life because it inhibits photosynthesis and increases mutation rates in DNA and damages epidermal tissues in plants and animals.

BIOTA OF THE ARCTIC

A transition zone exists at the northern limit of trees where coniferous forest interdigitates with treeless tundra vegetation. In North America, white and black spruce (*Picea glauca* and *P. mariana*) interface with tundra, whereas in Siberia and northern Europe larch (*Larix*) is the primary tree line species. Cottonwoods (*Populus* species) often penetrate the tundra landscape in the Low Arctic along major rivers. Major vegetation types of the Low Arctic include low-shrub tundra, dominated by species of willow

(*Salix*) and dwarf birch (*Betula*); tall-shrub tundra, dominated by species of willow, shrub birch, and alder (*Alnus*); and combinations of sedges and dwarf shrubs, such as species of Labrador tea (*Ledum*), blueberry and cranberry (*Vaccinium*), crowberry (*Empetrum*), and Arctic heather (*Cassiope*), in wetter sites. Cushion plants (*Dryas* and *Saxifraga* species) are common on windswept uplands. Lichens and mosses are important components of the ground cover in some areas. In the Low Arctic, most land surfaces are fully vegetated, with the exception of rock outcrops, dry ridge tops, river gravel bars, and scree slopes (those slopes that have an accumulation of rocky debris at the angle of repose).

The vegetation of the High Arctic is less rich than that of the Low Arctic, containing only about half the vascular plant species found in the Low Arctic. For example, more than 600 species of plants are found in the Low Arctic of North America, but in the extreme High Arctic of northern Ellesmere Island and Greenland—north of 83° N—fewer than 100 species of vascular plants grow. The shorter growing season, cooler summers, and drier conditions, as well as the distance of these landmasses from continental flora, account for this difference. More than 40 percent of vascular plant species of the Arctic are circumpolar in distribution. Mosses increase in importance in High Arctic plant communities, and shrub species decrease markedly, with only a few prostrate willows, dwarf birch, and other dwarf shrubs remaining. Prostrate willows, however, remain important components of plant communities that retain some winter snow cover, even in the northernmost land areas. Sedge-moss meadows occur on limited wet sites in valley bottoms watered by melting snows. Upland sites are drier and have a more sparse ground cover that merges into polar desert at higher elevations or where insufficient moisture is available for plant growth. Grasses, occasional prostrate willows, and mat-forming dryas occur in patches in the uplands and are the dominant vegetation in the polar barrens.

The true polar desert generally occurs on coastal areas fringing the Arctic Ocean and on areas of a few hundred metres elevation in the extreme High Arctic where soils have not developed and the frost-free period and soil moisture are insufficient for most plant growth. The occasional plants growing there often become established in frost cracks that capture blowing snow and finer windblown soil material. Plants adapted to these conditions include species of the Arctic poppy (*Papaver*), some rushes (*Juncus*), small saxifrages (*Saxifraga*), and a few other rosette-forming herbaceous species. The Arctic poppy and a few of the other flowering herbs adapted to the High Arctic have flowers that are solartropic (turning in response to the Sun). Their parabolic-shaped blossoms track daily movements of the Sun, thereby concentrating solar heat on the developing ovary, warming pollinating insects that land there, and speeding the growth of embryonic seeds.

Arctic ecosystems lack the diversity and richness of species that characterize temperate and tropical ecosystems. Animal as well as plant species decline in number with increasing latitude in both polar regions. Vertebrate species of the Arctic tundra and polar barrens are limited to mammals and birds; no amphibians or reptiles occur there. About 20 species of mammals and more than 100 species of birds are present throughout the Arctic. Most are circumpolar in their distribution as single species or closely related species; for example, the caribou of North America and the domestic and wild reindeer of Eurasia belong to the same species, *Rangifer tarandus*, whereas the

Grizzly bear (Ursus arctos horribilis). Stephen J. Krasemann/Peter Arnold, Inc.

lemmings of the Eurasian Arctic are a closely related but distinct species from those of northern North America and Greenland. This similarity in Arctic mammalian fauna is a result of the lower sea levels of the Pleistocene glaciations, when a broad land connection, known as the Bering Land Bridge, connected present-day Alaska and Siberia.

Some Arctic mammalian fauna—primarily herbivores such as caribou and reindeer, muskox (*Ovibos moschatus*), and Arctic fox (*Alopex lagopus*), and species of Arctic hare (*Lepus*) and collared and brown lemmings (*Dicrostonyx* and *Lemmus*)—rarely occur outside the Arctic and are adapted to life in this environment. Other fauna such as species of ground squirrel (*Spermophilus*), vole (*Microtus*), shrew (family Soricidae), and red fox (*Vulpes*), as well as ermine (*Mustela erminea*), wolverine (*Gulo gulo*), wolf (*Canis lupus*), and brown bear (*Ursus arctos*) are common to other ecosystems but are distributed widely throughout the Arctic. A few other typical temperate species have penetrated northward into the Low Arctic where suitable habitat is available. The moose (*Alces alces*) and snowshoe hare (*Lepus americanus*) in North America are examples, and their movement into the Low Arctic may be a consequence of a warming climate and an increase of willows and other shrubs, especially in riparian habitats. Where mountain ranges in boreal forest regions continue into the Arctic—as they do in northwestern North America and Siberia—species of mountain sheep (*Ovis*) and marmots (*Marmota*), typical of the alpine zone, have extended their distribution into the Arctic.

On land areas of the extreme High Arctic, above 80° N, which include only parts of Axel Heiberg and Ellesmere

Wolverine (Gulo gulo). Alan G. Nelson/Root Resources

islands in the Canadian Arctic, northernmost Greenland, northern portions of Svalbard, and Franz Josef Land, only a few mammal species are able to maintain viable populations. In the Canadian High Arctic the musk ox, Peary caribou, Arctic hare, and collared lemming are the only mammalian herbivores, and their predators, the wolf, Arctic fox, wolverine, and ermine, are also present. In northern Greenland these same species are found, with caribou and possibly the wolverine being absent in historical times. Only caribou and the Arctic fox are native to Svalbard, and only the Arctic fox is present on Franz Josef Land. In all these High Arctic areas the polar bear (*Ursus maritimus*), a creature of the sea ice that preys largely on seals, may occasionally be found on land, where females

"White" phase of Arctic fox changing to its summer coat. Russ Kinne — Photo Researchers/EB Inc.

den to bear young or where they graze (rarely) the vegetation or prey on land mammals or nesting birds.

Terrestrial avian fauna of the Arctic includes only a few resident species, among them the ptarmigan (*Lagopus* species), snowy owl (*Nyctea scandiaca*), gyrfalcon (*Falco rusticolus*), and raven (*Corvus corax*); the remaining species are present in the Arctic only in summer to breed and rear young, migrating to temperate, tropical, or maritime areas of more southern latitudes during winter. Although the ability to fly has allowed birds to occupy isolated and insular habitats within the Arctic that have been largely inaccessible to mammals, their distribution throughout the Arctic has been tied closely to the location of their wintering areas and annual migration routes. These migration routes, especially those of shorebirds and waterfowl, often follow the coastlines of continents, yet some species cross extensive bodies of water. Nevertheless, the North Atlantic Ocean offers a partial barrier to the circumpolar mixing of species, and thus there is greater similarity between the avian fauna of the Arctic of western North America and eastern Eurasia than there is among the species of the Arctic areas of Europe, eastern North America, and Greenland.

Shorebirds, waterfowl, and passerine species of the family Fringillidae (finches, buntings, and sparrows) are the most abundant species nesting in the Arctic. Wet sedge meadows often associated with lake margins, estuaries, and seacoasts are favoured nesting habitats of shorebirds and waterfowl. Nesting densities of passerine species are highest in shrub communities at the southern margins of the tundra and in riparian habitats; they decline rapidly in the High Arctic. Only the redpoll (*Acanthis* species) and snow bunting (*Plectrophenax nivalis*) among this group extend their range to the northernmost land areas.

Golden eagle (Aquila chrysaetos). © Alan and Sandy Carey

In addition to resident species, raptorial birds that commonly nest in the Arctic include the peregrine falcon (*Falco peregrinus*), rough-legged hawk (*Buteo lagopus*), short-eared owl (*Asio flammeus*), and, in mountainous terrain, the golden eagle (*Aguila chrysaetos*) in North America and the white-tailed eagle (*Italiacetus albicilla*) in Greenland and Eurasia. The jaegers (*Stercorarius* species), which spend the major part of their lives at sea during most of the year, nest in tundra and polar barrens and prey on lemmings and eggs and nestlings of other birds during the breeding season. Marine birds of the Procellariidae (fulmars), Laridae (gulls and terns), and Alcidae (puffins, murres, dovkies, and auklets) that are dependent on a marine food base often nest colonially on coastal cliffs in the Arctic. These nesting colonies are usually found adjacent to upwelling currents in the sea where invertebrates and fish that the birds feed on are most abundant. In the High Arctic, upwelling currents result in open water areas within the pack ice called polynya; these enable seabirds to feed and nest at latitudes above 75° N.

BIOTA OF THE ANTARCTIC

The flora of Antarctica consists mainly of soil and freshwater algae, lichens, mosses, fungi, and only two native species of vascular plants. The terrestrial fauna consists of a few invertebrate species of protozoans, rotifers, nematodes, tardigrades, collembola (primitive wingless insects), and a species of mite. These life-forms are restricted mainly to moist beds of moss. The diversity of marine mammals and birds in the coastal areas and associated pack ice is dependent on marine food chains in the adjacent seas.

In Antarctica unique endolithic (stone-dwelling) forms of life (cyanobacteria) occur within and just below the surface of porous rocks. These cyanobacteria can be found in dry valleys of southern Victoria Land, where they are adapted to remain dormant for extended periods until rare occasions when melting snow provides the moisture necessary for life processes. Although this is an extreme cold-desert environment, similar forms of life occur within rocks in hot deserts.

THE DEVELOPMENT AND STRUCTURE OF POPULATIONS AND COMMUNITIES IN POLAR ECOSYSTEMS

The low species diversity of both plants and animals in polar regions contributes to the lack of complexity that characterizes Arctic and Antarctic ecosystems. The short summer season during which plants can grow and insects and other invertebrates can be active contributes to the lower productivity and relative simplicity of these ecosystems. In addition, the cooler temperatures limit the rate at which soil nutrients essential for plant growth are released through decomposition of organic material, breakdown of the parent rock, and fixation of nitrogen by soil microbes.

A consequence of ecosystem simplicity is a lack of stability. Animals tend to undergo wide population fluctuations in the tundra and polar barrens. These fluctuations are stimulated by periodic extremes of weather and imbalances in herbivore-plant and predator-prey relationships. Each species plays a much more dominant role in the trophic dynamics of ecosystems in the Arctic than do species in the highly complex temperate and tropical ecosystems. The extreme abundance of lemmings during the peak of their population cycle (as many as 200 per hectare) is accompanied by high reproductive success and rapid increase of their predators—Arctic foxes, ermines, snowy owls, and other species. Conversely, when lemming numbers are low (fewer than 1 per hectare) breeding among their predators ceases and predator populations plummet.

In the High Arctic, animal populations live close to their biological limitations. Peary caribou or musk oxen may be so affected by periods of extreme weather that they become locally extinct. Reestablishment of the species may not occur until favourable conditions allow adjacent populations to build up, an event that may take decades. Indeed, in northernmost Greenland, although caribou have not been present in recent history, antlers and bones indicate their periodic presence at least 7,000 years ago.

Snow plays an important role in determining the characteristics and distribution of plant and animal communities in tundra and polar barrens. Winters are long, and the limited snow that falls usually accumulates without melting throughout the entire season. The snow cover, however, is not stable. The strong winds that characterize these treeless landscapes redistribute the snow, removing it from landscape convexities and depositing it as drifts in concavities, in patches of shrubs, or leeward of ridge tops and boulders. The wind also compacts snow, increasing its density, thus enabling animals to move more easily over its surface while hampering their ability to dig through to find food below. Snow, therefore, influences the location, food selection, and energy expenditure of large herbivores that must move across the winter landscape to feed. Areas of deeper snow cover appeal to small rodents who feed and construct winter nests at the ground's surface under the insulating layer of snow.

The pattern of distribution of snow on the tundra and polar barrens is also a major determinant in the distribution of vegetation. Most plants require snow cover to protect them from the extreme cold and drying conditions of winter. Areas in which the snow cover has been blown away are the first to initiate plant growth in summer, whereas those in which snowbanks are slow to melt support only those plants adapted to the shorter snow-free season. The winter accumulation of snow, however, is often the primary source of moisture for the summer growth of plants. Consequently, windy exposures with little snow cover often suffer summer drought that limits plant growth, whereas snow-bed plant communities are well watered throughout summer.

BIOLOGICAL PRODUCTIVITY IN POLAR ECOSYSTEMS

In the Low Arctic, vegetation covers 80 to 100 percent of the land area. The rapid growth of vascular plants under the continuous daylight of the brief Arctic summer is the basis for the relatively high productivity of these plant communities at such high altitudes. Because all aboveground productivity of plants is close to ground level in the tundra in contrast to forest biomes, it is readily available to vertebrate herbivores. As a consequence large concentrations of caribou and geese graze locally in the Low Arctic in summer but migrate out of the Arctic to winter when the quality of forage declines and its availability is limited by the wind-packed snow cover. Although tundra systems experience a burst of plant and animal productivity during the brief Arctic summer, only a few animal species remain active in the Arctic throughout the long winter. Herbivores are dependent on plant production of the previous summer, and carnivores depend on their herbivore prey. Total annual productivity in the tundra and polar barrens is several orders of magnitude less than it is in most temperate or tropical ecosystems.

Vertebrate herbivory may result in changes in tundra vegetation through selective feeding on preferred plant species, trampling, and recycling of soil nutrients through excretion. Where caribou, musk oxen, lemmings, and geese concentrate their grazing activity they may actually increase production of tundra vegetation. This results from removal of much of the annual vegetative growth, exposing the underlying new growth of plants to the rays of the sun and the soil to increased heating, and from speeding up the recycling of organic material through digestion and excretion that releases nutrients to the soil.

CHAPTER 5
AQUATIC ECOSYSTEM CASE STUDIES

E cosystems are found on land and in the water. The latter occur along Earth's many coastlines or in watery areas farther inland. The water of which such aquatic ecosystems are comprised can be saline or fresh, moving or still. A sampling of the various types of aquatic ecosystems is offered in this chapter, along with a discussion of boundary ecosystems, which are biogeographic areas that, in addition to acting as a boundary between two terrestrial ecosystems, straddle different aquatic systems and exist between aquatic and terrestrial environments.

THE MARINE ECOSYSTEM

Marine waters cover two-thirds of the surface of the Earth. In some places the ocean is deeper than Mount Everest is high; for example, the Mariana Trench and the Tonga Trench in the western part of the Pacific Ocean reach depths in excess of 10,000 metres (32,800 feet). Within this ocean habitat live a wide variety of organisms that have evolved in response to various features of their environs.

THE ORIGINS OF MARINE LIFE

The Earth formed approximately 4.6 billion years ago. As it cooled, water in the atmosphere condensed and the Earth was pummeled with torrential rains, which filled its great basins, forming seas. The primeval atmosphere and waters harboured the inorganic components hydrogen, methane, ammonia, and water. These substances are thought to have combined to form the first organic compounds when sparked by electrical discharges of lightning.

Some of the earliest known organisms are cyanobacteria (formerly referred to as blue-green algae). Evidence of these early photosynthetic prokaryotes has been found in Australia in Precambrian marine sediments called stromatolites that are approximately 3 billion years old. Although the diversity of life-forms observed in modern oceans did not appear until much later, during the Precambrian (4.6 billion to 542 million years ago) many kinds of bacteria, algae, protozoa, and primitive metazoa evolved to exploit the early marine habitats of the world. During the Cambrian Period (542 million to 488 million years ago) a major radiation of life occurred in the oceans. Fossils of familiar organisms such as cnidaria (e.g., jellyfish), echinoderms (e.g., feather stars), precursors of the fishes (e.g., the protochordate *Pikaia* from the Burgess Shale of Canada), and other vertebrates are found in marine sediments of this age.

The first fossil fishes are found in sediments from the Ordovician Period (488 to 444 million years ago). Changes in the physical conditions of the ocean that are thought to have occurred in the Precambrian—an increase in the concentration of oxygen in seawater and a build-up of the ozone layer that reduced dangerous ultraviolet radiation—may have facilitated the increase and dispersal of living things.

THE SHAPE OF THE OCEANS

The shape of the oceans and seas of the world has changed significantly throughout the past 600 million years. According to the theory of plate tectonics, the crust of the Earth is made up of many dynamic plates. There are two types of plates—oceanic and continental—which float on the surface of the Earth's mantle, diverging, converging, or sliding against one another. When two plates diverge, magma from the mantle wells up and cools, forming new crust. When convergence occurs, one plate descends—i.e., is subducted—below the other and crust is resorbed into the mantle. Examples of both processes are observed in the marine environment. Oceanic crust is created along oceanic ridges or rift areas, which are vast undersea mountain ranges such as the Mid-Atlantic Ridge. Excess crust is reabsorbed along subduction zones, which usually are marked by deep-sea trenches such as the Kuril Trench off the coast of Japan.

The shape of the ocean also is altered as sea levels change. During ice ages a higher proportion of the waters of the Earth is bound in the polar ice caps, resulting in a relatively low sea level. When the polar ice caps melt during interglacial periods, the sea level rises. These changes in sea level cause great changes in the distribution of marine environments such as coral reefs. For example, during the last Pleistocene Ice Age the Great Barrier Reef did not exist as it does today; the continental shelf on which the reef now is found was above the high-tide mark.

Marine organisms are not distributed evenly throughout the oceans. Variations in characteristics of the marine environment create different habitats and influence what types of organisms will inhabit them. The availability of light, water depth, proximity to land, and topographic complexity all affect marine habitats. The availability of light affects which organisms can inhabit a certain area of a marine ecosystem. The greater the depth of the water, the less light can penetrate until below a certain depth there is no light whatsoever. This area of inky darkness, which occupies the great bulk of the ocean, is called the aphotic zone. The illuminated region above it is called the photic zone, within which are distinguished the euphotic and disphotic zones. The euphotic zone is the layer closer to the surface that receives enough light for photosynthesis to occur. Beneath lies the disphotic zone, which is illuminated but so poorly that rates of respiration exceed those of photosynthesis.

The actual depth of these zones depends on local conditions of cloud cover, water turbidity, and ocean surface. In general, the euphotic zone can extend to depths of 80 to 100 metres (about 260 to 330 feet) and the disphotic zone to depths of 80 to 700 metres (about 260 to 2,300 feet). Marine organisms are particularly abundant in the photic zone, especially the euphotic portion; however, many organisms inhabit the aphotic zone and migrate vertically to the photic zone every night. Other organisms, such as the tripod fish and some species of sea cucumbers and brittle stars, remain in darkness all their lives.

Marine environments can be characterized broadly as a water, or pelagic, environment and a bottom, or benthic,

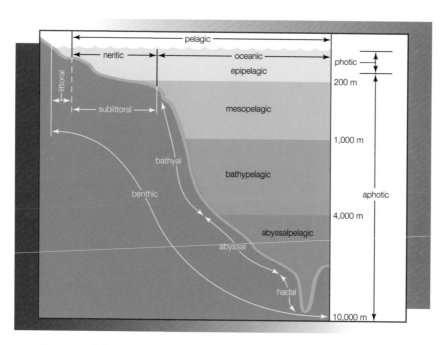

Zonation of the ocean. Note that in the littoral zone the water is at the high-tide mark. Encyclopædia Britannica, Inc.

environment. Within the pelagic environment the waters are divided into the neritic province, which includes the water above the continental shelf, and the oceanic province, which includes all the open waters beyond the continental shelf. The high nutrient levels of the neritic province—resulting from dissolved materials in riverine runoff—distinguish this province from the oceanic. The upper portion of both the neritic and oceanic waters—the epipelagic zone—is where photosynthesis occurs; it is roughly equivalent to the photic zone. Below this zone lie the mesopelagic, ranging between 200 and 1,000 metres (about 660 to 3,300 feet), the bathypelagic, from 1,000 to 4,000 metres (about 3,300 to 13,100 feet), and the abyssalpelagic, which encompasses the deepest parts of the oceans from 4,000 metres to the recesses of the deep-sea trenches. The benthic environment also is divided into different zones. The supralittoral is above the high-tide mark and is usually not under water. The intertidal, or littoral, zone ranges from the high-tide mark (the maximum elevation of the tide) to the shallow, offshore waters. The sublittoral is the environment beyond the low-tide mark and is often used to refer to substrata of the continental shelf, which reaches depths of between 150 and 300 metres (500 and 1,000 feet). Sediments of the continental shelf that influence marine organisms generally originate from the land, particularly in the form of riverine runoff, and include clay, silt, and sand. Beyond the continental shelf is the bathyal zone, which occurs at depths of 150 to 4,000 metres (500 to 13,100 feet) and includes the descending continental slope and rise. The abyssal zone (between 4,000 and 6,000 metres [13,100 and 19,800 feet]) represents a substantial portion of the oceans. The deepest region of the oceans (greater than 6,000 metres) is the hadal zone of the deep-sea trenches. Sediments of the deep sea primarily originate from a rain of dead marine organisms and their wastes.

THE PHYSICAL AND CHEMICAL PROPERTIES OF SEAWATER

The physical and chemical properties of seawater vary according to latitude, depth, nearness to land, and input of fresh water. Approximately 3.5 percent of seawater is composed of dissolved compounds, while the other 96.5 percent is pure water. The chemical composition of seawater reflects such processes as erosion of rock and sediments, volcanic activity, gas exchange with the atmosphere, the metabolic and breakdown products of organisms, and rain. In addition to carbon, the nutrients essential for living organisms include nitrogen and phosphorus, which are minor constituents of seawater and thus are often limiting factors in organic cycles of the ocean. Concentrations of phosphorus and nitrogen are generally low in the photic zone because they are rapidly taken up by marine organisms. The highest concentrations of these nutrients generally are found below 500 metres (1,640 feet), a result of the decay of organisms.

Other important elements include silicon, which commonly occurs in nature as silicon dioxide (SiO_2) and is also called silica. It cycles through the marine environment, entering primarily through riverine runoff. Silica is removed from the ocean by organisms such as diatoms and radiolarians that use an amorphous form of silica in their cell walls. After they die, their skeletons settle through the water column and the silica redissolves. A small number reach the ocean floor, where they either remain, forming a silaceous ooze, or dissolve and are returned to the photic zone by upwelling. Calcium, essential in the skeletons of many organisms such as fish and corals, also are present.

The chemical composition of the atmosphere also affects that of the ocean. For example, carbon dioxide is absorbed by the ocean and oxygen is released to the

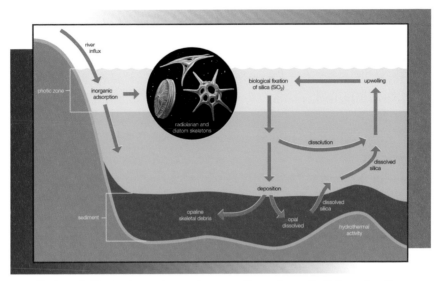

Cycling of silica in the marine environment. Encyclopædia Britannica, Inc.

atmosphere through the activities of marine plants. The dumping of pollutants into the sea also can affect the chemical makeup of the ocean, contrary to earlier assumptions that, for example, toxins could be safely disposed of there.

The physical and chemical properties of seawater have a great effect on organisms, varying especially with the size of the creature. As an example, seawater is viscous to very small animals (less than 1 mm [0.04 inch] long) such as ciliates but not to large marine creatures such as tuna.

Marine organisms have evolved a wide variety of unique physiological and morphological features that allow them to live in the sea. Notothenid fishes in Antarctica are able to inhabit waters as cold as -2 °C (28 °F) because of proteins in their blood that act as antifreeze. Many organisms are able to achieve neutral buoyancy by secreting gas into internal chambers, as cephalopods do, or into swim bladders, as some fish do. Other organisms use lipids, which are less dense than water, to achieve this effect. Some animals, especially those in the aphotic zone, generate light to attract prey. Animals in the disphotic zone such as hatchetfish produce light by means of organs called photophores to break up the silhouette of their bodies and avoid visual detection by predators. Many marine animals can detect vibrations or sound in the water over great distances by means of specialized organs. Certain fishes have lateral-line systems, which they use to detect prey, and whales have a sound-producing organ called a melon with which they communicate.

Tolerance to differences in salinity varies greatly. Stenohaline organisms have a low tolerance to salinity changes, whereas euryhaline organisms, which are found in areas where river and sea meet (estuaries), are very tolerant of large changes in salinity. Euryhaline organisms are also very tolerant of changes in temperature. Animals that migrate between fresh water and salt water, such as salmon or eels, are capable of controlling their osmotic environment by active pumping or the retention of salts. Body architecture varies greatly in marine waters. The body shape of the cnidarian by-the-wind-sailor (*Velella velella*)—an animal that lives on the surface of the water (pleuston) and sails with the assistance of a modified flotation chamber—contrasts sharply with the sleek, elongated shape of the barracuda.

OCEAN CURRENTS

The movements of ocean waters are influenced by numerous factors, including the rotation of the Earth (which is responsible for the Coriolis effect), atmospheric circulation patterns that influence surface waters, and temperature and salinity gradients between the tropics and the polar regions (thermohaline circulation). The resultant patterns of circulation range from those that cover great areas, such as the North Subtropical Gyre, which follows a path thousands of kilometres long, to small-scale turbulences of less than one metre.

Marine organisms of all sizes are influenced by these patterns, which can determine the range of a species. For example, krill (*Euphausia superba*) are restricted to the Antarctic Circumpolar Current. Distribution patterns of both large and small pelagic organisms are affected as well. Mainstream currents such as the Gulf Stream and East Australian Current transport larvae great distances. As a result cold temperate coral reefs receive a tropical infusion when fish and invertebrate larvae from the tropics are relocated to high latitudes by these currents. The successful recruitment of eels to Europe depends on the strength of the Gulf Stream to transport them from spawning sites in the Caribbean. Areas where the ocean is affected by nearshore features, such as estuaries, or areas in which there is a vertical salinity gradient (halocline) often exhibit intense biological activity. In these environments, small organisms can become concentrated, providing a rich supply of food for other animals.

Marine Biota

Marine biota can be classified broadly into those organisms living in either the pelagic environment (plankton and nekton) or the benthic environment (benthos). Some organisms, however, are benthic in one stage of life and pelagic in another. Producers that synthesize organic molecules exist in both environments. Single-celled or multicelled plankton with photosynthetic pigments are the producers of the photic zone in the pelagic environment. Typical benthic producers are microalgae (e.g., diatoms), macroalgae (e.g., the kelp *Macrocystis pyrifera*), or sea grass (e.g., *Zostera*).

Plankton are the numerous, primarily microscopic inhabitants of the pelagic environment. They are critical components of food chains in all marine environments because they provide nutrition for the nekton (e.g., crustaceans, fish, and squid) and benthos (e.g., sea squirts and sponges). They also exert a global effect on the biosphere because the balance of components of the Earth's atmosphere depends to a great extent on the photosynthetic activities of some plankton.

The term "plankton" is derived from the Greek *planktos*, meaning wandering or drifting, an apt description of

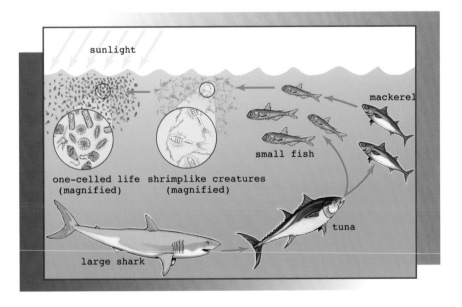

Diatoms and other phytoplankton form the foundations of ocean food chains. Shrimplike krill consume the phytoplankton, and small fishes eat the krill. At the top of the food chain, dining on these smaller fishes, are larger, predatory fishes. Encyclopædia Britannica, Inc.

the way most plankton spend their existence, floating with the ocean's currents. Not all plankton, however, are unable to control their movements, and many forms depend on self-directed motions for their survival.

Plankton range in size from tiny microbes (1 micrometre [0.000039 inch] or less) to jellyfish whose gelatinous bell can reach up to 2 metres (about 7 feet) in width and whose tentacles can extend over 15 metres (about 50 feet). However, most planktonic organisms, called plankters, are less than 1 mm (0.04 inch) long. These microbes thrive on nutrients in seawater and are often photosynthetic. The plankton include a wide variety of organisms such as algae, bacteria, protozoans, the larvae of some animals, and crustaceans. A large proportion of the plankton are protists—i.e., eukaryotic, predominantly single-celled organisms. Plankton can be broadly divided into phytoplankton, which are plants or plantlike protists; zooplankton, which are animals or animal-like protists; and microbes such as bacteria. Phytoplankton carry out photosynthesis and are the producers of the marine community; zooplankton are the heterotrophic consumers.

Diatoms and dinoflagellates (approximate range between 15 and 1,000 micrometres [0.0006 and 0.04 inch] in length) are two highly diverse groups of photosynthetic protists that are important components of the plankton. Diatoms are the most abundant phytoplankton. While many dinoflagellates carry out photosynthesis, some also consume bacteria or algae. Other important groups of protists include flagellates, foraminiferans, radiolarians, acantharians, and ciliates. Many of these protists are important consumers and a food source for zooplankton.

Zooplankton, which are greater than 0.05 mm (0.002 inch) in size, are divided into two general categories: meroplankton, which spend only a part of their life cycle—usually the larval or juvenile stage—as plankton, and holoplankton, which exist as plankton all their lives. Many larval meroplankton in coastal, oceanic, and even freshwater environments (including sea urchins, intertidal snails, and crabs, lobsters, and fish) bear little or no resemblance to their adult forms. These larvae may exhibit features unique to the larval stage, such as the spectacular spiny armour on the larvae of certain crustaceans (e.g., *Squilla*), probably used to ward off predators.

Important holoplanktonic animals include such lobsterlike crustaceans as the copepods, cladocerans, and euphausids (krill), which are important components of the marine environment because they serve as food sources for fish and marine mammals. Gelatinous forms such as larvaceans, salps, and siphonophores graze on phytoplankton or other zooplankton. Some omnivorous zooplankton such as euphausids and some copepods consume both phytoplankton and zooplankton; their feeding behaviour changes according to the availability and type of prey. The grazing and predatory activity of some zooplankton can be so intense that measurable reductions in phytoplankton or zooplankton abundance (or biomass) occur. For example, when jellyfish occur in high concentration in enclosed seas, they may consume such large numbers of fish larvae as to greatly reduce fish populations.

The jellylike plankton are numerous and predatory. They secure their prey with stinging cells (nematocysts) or sticky cells (colloblasts of comb jellies). Large numbers of the Portuguese man-of-war (*Physalia*), with its conspicuous gas bladder, the by-the-wind-sailor (*Velella velella*), and the small blue disk-shaped *Porpita porpita* are propelled along the surface by the wind, and after strong onshore winds they may be found strewn on the beach. Beneath the surface, comb jellies often abound, as do siphonophores, salps, and scyphomedusae.

The pelagic environment was once thought to present few distinct habitats, in contrast to the array of niches within the benthic environment. Because of its apparent uniformity, the pelagic realm was understood to be distinguished simply by plankton of different sizes. Small-scale variations in the pelagic environment, however, have been discovered that affect biotic distributions. Living and dead matter form organic aggregates called marine snow to which members of the plankton community may adhere, producing patchiness in biotic distributions. Marine snow includes structures such as aggregates of cells and mucus as well as drifting macroalgae and other flotsam that range in size from 0.5 mm to 1 cm (0.02 to 0.4 inch), although these aggregates can be as small as 0.05 mm and as large as 100 cm (39 inches). Many types of microbes, phytoplankton, and zooplankton stick to marine snow, and some grazing copepods and predators will feed from the surface of these structures. Marine snow is extremely abundant at times, particularly after plankton blooms. Significant quantities of organic material from upper layers of the ocean may sink to the ocean floor as marine snow, providing an important source of food for bottom dwellers. Other structures that plankton respond to in the marine environment include aggregates of phytoplankton cells that form large rafts in tropical and temperate waters of the world (e.g., cells of *Oscillatoria* [*Trichodesmium*] *erthraeus*) and various types of seaweed (e.g., *Sargassum*, *Phyllospora*, *Macrocystis*) that detach from the sea floor and drift.

NEKTON

Nekton are the active swimmers of the oceans and are often the best-known organisms of marine waters. Nekton are the top predators in most marine food chains. The distinction between nekton and plankton is not always sharp. As mentioned above, many large marine animals, such as marlin and tuna, spend the larval stage of their lives as plankton and their adult stage as large and active members of the nekton. Other organisms such as krill are referred to as both micronekton and macrozooplankton.

The vast majority of nekton are vertebrates (e.g., fishes, reptiles, and mammals), mollusks, and crustaceans. The most numerous group of nekton are the fishes, with approximately 16,000 species. Nekton are found at all depths and latitudes of marine waters. Whales, penguins, seals, and icefish abound in polar waters. Lantern fish (family Myctophidae) are common in the aphotic zone along with gulpers (*Saccopharynx*), whalefish (family Cetomimidae), seven-gilled sharks, and others. Nekton diversity is greatest in tropical waters, where in particular there are large numbers of fish species.

The largest animals on the Earth, the blue whales (*Balaenoptera musculus*), which grow to 25 to 30 metres (about 80 to 100 feet) long, are members of the nekton. These huge mammals and other baleen whales (order Mysticeti), which are distinguished by fine filtering plates in their mouths, feed on plankton and micronekton as do whale sharks (*Rhinocodon typus*), the largest fish in the world (usually 12 to 14 metres [about 39 to 46 feet] long, with some reaching 17 metres [about 56 feet]). The largest carnivores that consume large prey include the toothed whales (order Odontoceti—for example, the killer whales, *Orcinus orca*), great white sharks (*Carcharodon carcharias*), tiger sharks (*Galeocerdo cuvieri*), black marlin (*Makaira indica*), bluefin tuna (*Thunnus thynnus*), and giant groupers (*Epinephelus lanceolatus*).

Nekton form the basis of important fisheries around the world. Vast schools of small anchovies, herring, and

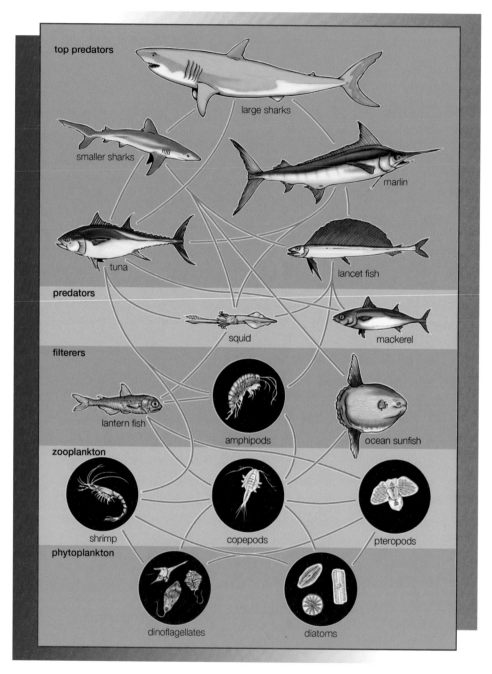

top predators

large sharks

smaller sharks

marlin

tuna

lancet fish

predators

squid

mackerel

filterers

lantern fish

amphipods

ocean sunfish

zooplankton

shrimp

copepods

pteropods

phytoplankton

dinoflagellates

diatoms

Generalized aquatic food web. Parasites, among the most diverse species in the food web, are not shown. Encyclopædia Britannica, Inc.

sardines generally account for one-quarter to one-third of the annual harvest from the ocean. Squid are also economically valuable nekton. Halibut, sole, and cod are demersal (i.e., bottom-dwelling) fish that are commercially important as food for humans. They are generally caught in continental shelf waters. Because pelagic nekton often abound in areas of upwelling where the waters are nutrient-rich, these regions also are major fishing areas.

BENTHOS

Organisms are abundant in surface sediments of the continental shelf and in deeper waters, with a great diversity found in or on sediments. In shallow waters, beds of seagrass provide a rich habitat for polychaete worms, crustaceans (e.g., amphipods), and fishes. On the surface of and within intertidal sediments most animal activities are influenced strongly by the state of the tide. On many sediments in the photic zone, however, the only photosynthetic organisms are microscopic benthic diatoms.

Benthic organisms can be classified according to size. The macrobenthos are those organisms larger than 1 mm (0.04 inch). Those that eat organic material in sediments are called deposit feeders (e.g., holothurians, echinoids, gastropods), those that feed on the plankton above are the suspension feeders (e.g., bivalves, ophiuroids, crinoids), and those that consume other fauna in the benthic assemblage are predators (e.g., starfish, gastropods). Organisms between 0.1 and 1 mm (0.004 and 0.04 inch) constitute the meiobenthos. These larger microbes, which include foraminiferans, turbellarians, and polychaetes, frequently dominate benthic food chains, filling the roles of nutrient recycler, decomposer, primary producer, and predator. The microbenthos are those organisms smaller than 1 mm; they include diatoms, bacteria, and ciliates.

Organic matter is decomposed aerobically by bacteria near the surface of the sediment where oxygen is abundant. The consumption of oxygen at this level, however, deprives deeper layers of oxygen, and marine sediments below the surface layer are anaerobic. The thickness of the oxygenated layer varies according to grain size, which determines how permeable the sediment is to oxygen and the amount of organic matter it contains. As oxygen concentration diminishes, anaerobic processes come to dominate. The transition layer between oxygen-rich and oxygen-poor layers is called the redox discontinuity layer and appears as a gray layer above the black anaerobic layers. Organisms have evolved various ways of coping with the lack of oxygen. Some anaerobes release hydrogen sulfide, ammonia, and other toxic reduced ions through metabolic processes. The thiobiota, made up primarily of microorganisms, metabolize sulfur. Most organisms that live below the redox layer, however, have to create an aerobic environment for themselves. Burrowing animals generate a respiratory current along their burrow systems to oxygenate their dwelling places; the influx of oxygen must be constantly maintained because the surrounding anoxic layer quickly depletes the burrow of oxygen. Many bivalves (e.g., *Mya arenaria*) extend long siphons upward into oxygenated waters near the surface so that they can respire and feed while remaining sheltered from predation deep in the sediment. Many large mollusks use a muscular "foot" to dig with, and in some cases they use it to propel themselves away from predators such as starfish. The consequent "irrigation" of burrow systems can create oxygen and nutrient fluxes that stimulate the production of benthic producers (e.g., diatoms).

Not all benthic organisms live within the sediment; certain benthic assemblages live on a rocky substrate.

Various phyla of algae—Rhodophyta (red), Chlorophyta (green), and Phaeophyta (brown)—are abundant and diverse in the photic zone on rocky substrata and are important producers. In intertidal regions algae are most abundant and largest near the low-tide mark. Ephemeral algae such as *Ulva*, *Enteromorpha*, and coralline algae cover a broad range of the intertidal. The mix of algae species found in any particular locale is dependent on latitude and also varies greatly according to wave exposure and the activity of grazers. For example, *Ascophyllum* spores cannot attach to rock in even a gentle ocean surge; as a result this plant is largely restricted to sheltered shores. The fastest-growing plant—adding as much as 1 metre per day to its length—is the giant kelp, *Macrocystis pyrifera*, which is found on subtidal rocky reefs. These plants, which may exceed 30 metres (100 feet) in length, characterize benthic habitats on many temperate reefs. Large laminarian and fucoid algae are also common on temperate rocky reefs, along with the encrusting (e.g., *Lithothamnion*) or short tufting forms (e.g., *Pterocladia*). Many algae on rocky reefs are harvested for food, fertilizer, and pharmaceuticals. Macroalgae are relatively rare on tropical reefs where corals abound, but *Sargassum* and a diverse assemblage of short filamentous and tufting algae are found, especially at the reef crest. Sessile and slow-moving invertebrates are common on reefs. In the intertidal and subtidal regions herbivorous gastropods and urchins abound and can have a great influence on the distribution of algae. Barnacles are common sessile animals in the intertidal. In the subtidal regions, sponges, ascidians, urchins, and anemones are particularly common where light levels drop and current speeds are high. Sessile assemblages of animals are often rich and diverse in caves and under boulders.

Reef-building coral polyps (Scleractinia) are organisms of the phylum Cnidaria that create a calcareous substrate upon which a diverse array of organisms live. Approximately 700 species of corals are found in the Pacific and Indian oceans and belong to genera such as *Porites*, *Acropora*, and *Montipora*. Some of the world's most complex ecosystems are found on coral reefs. Zooxanthellae are the photosynthetic, single-celled algae that live symbiotically within the tissue of corals and help to build the solid calcium carbonate matrix of the reef. Reef-building corals are found only in waters warmer than 18 °C (about 64 °F); warm temperatures are necessary, along with high light intensity, for the coral-algae complex to secrete calcium carbonate. Many tropical islands are composed entirely of hundreds of metres of coral built atop volcanic rock.

LINKS BETWEEN THE PELAGIC ENVIRONMENTS AND THE BENTHOS

Considering the pelagic and benthic environments in isolation from each other should be done cautiously because the two are interlinked in many ways. For example, pelagic plankton are an important source of food for animals on soft or rocky bottoms. Suspension feeders such as anemones and barnacles filter living and dead particles from the surrounding water while detritus feeders graze on the accumulation of particulate material raining from the water column above. The molts of crustaceans, plankton feces, dead plankton, and marine snow all contribute to this rain of fallout from the pelagic environment to the ocean bottom. This fallout can be so intense in certain weather patterns—such as the El Niño condition—that benthic animals on soft bottoms are smothered and die.

There also is variation in the rate of fallout of the plankton according to seasonal cycles of production. This variation can create seasonality in the abiotic zone where there is little or no variation in temperature or light. Plankton form marine sediments, and many types of fossilized protistan plankton, such as foraminiferans and coccoliths, are used to determine the age and origin of rocks.

ORGANISMS OF THE DEEP-SEA VENTS

Producers were discovered in the aphotic zone when exploration of the deep sea by submarine became common in the 1970s. Deep-sea hydrothermal vents now are known to be relatively common in areas of tectonic activity (e.g., spreading ridges). The vents are a nonphotosynthetic source of organic carbon available to organisms. A diversity of deep-sea organisms including mussels, large bivalve clams, and vestimentiferan worms are supported by bacteria that oxidize sulfur (sulfide) and derive chemical energy from the reaction. These organisms are referred to as chemoautotrophic, or chemosynthetic, as opposed to photosynthetic, organisms. Many of the species in the vent fauna have developed symbiotic relationships with chemoautotrophic bacteria, and as a consequence the megafauna are principally responsible for the primary production in the vent assemblage. The situation is analogous to that found on coral reefs where individual coral polyps have symbiotic relationships with zooxanthellae.

In addition to symbiotic bacteria there is a rich assemblage of free-living bacteria around vents. For example, *Beggiatoas*-like bacteria often form conspicuous weblike mats on any hard surface; these mats have been shown to have chemoautotrophic metabolism. Large numbers of brachyuran (e.g., *Bythograea*) and galatheid crabs, large sea anemones (e.g., *Actinostola callasi*), copepods, other plankton, and some fish—especially the eelpout *Thermarces cerberus*—are found in association with vents.

The Distribution and Dispersal of Marine Organisms

The distribution patterns of marine organisms are influenced by physical and biological processes in both ecological time (tens of years) and geologic time (hundreds to millions of years). The shapes of the Earth's oceans have been influenced by plate tectonics, and as a consequence the distributions of fossil and extant marine organisms also have been affected. Vicariance theory argues that plate tectonics has a major role in determining biogeographic patterns. For example, Australia was once—90 million years ago—close to the South Pole and had few coral reefs. Since then Australia has been moving a few millimetres each year closer to the Equator. As a result of this movement and local oceanographic conditions, coral reef environments are extending ever so slowly southward.

Dispersal may also have an important role in biogeographic patterns of abundance. The importance of dispersal varies greatly with local oceanographic features, such as the direction and intensity of currents and the biology of the organisms. Humans can also have an impact on patterns of distribution and the extinction of marine organisms. For example, fishing intensity in the Irish Sea was based on catch limits set for cod with no regard for the biology of other species. One consequence of this practice was that the local skate, which had a slow reproductive rate, was quickly fished to extinction.

A characteristic of many marine organisms is a bipartite life cycle, which can affect the dispersal of an organism. Most animals found on soft and hard substrata, such as lobsters, crabs, barnacles, fish, polychaete worms, and sea urchins, spend their larval phase in the plankton, and in this phase are dispersed most widely. The length of the larval phase, which can vary from a few minutes to hundreds of days, has a major influence on dispersal. For example, wrasses of the genus *Thalassoma* have a long larval life, compared with many other types of reef fish, and populations of these fish are well dispersed to the reefs of isolated volcanic islands around the Pacific. The bipartite life cycle of algae also affects their dispersal, which occurs through algal spores. Although in general, spores disperse only a short distance from adult plants, limited swimming abilities—*Macrocystis* spores have flagella—and storms can disperse spores over greater distances.

MIGRATIONS OF MARINE ORGANISMS

The migrations of plankton and nekton throughout the water column in many parts of the world are well described. Diurnal vertical migrations are common. For example, some types of plankton, fish, and squid remain beneath the photic zone during the day, moving toward the surface after dusk and returning to the depths before dawn. It is generally argued that marine organisms migrate in response to light levels. This behaviour may be advantageous because by spending the daylight hours in the dim light or darkness beneath the photic zone plankton can avoid predators that locate their prey visually. After the Sun has set, plankton can rise to the surface waters where food is more abundant and where they can feed safely under the cover of darkness.

Larval forms can facilitate their horizontal transport along different currents by migrating vertically. This is possible because currents can differ in direction according to depth (e.g., above and below haloclines and thermoclines), as is the case in estuaries.

In coastal waters many larger invertebrates (e.g., mysids, amphipods, and polychaete worms) leave the cover of algae and sediments to migrate into the water column at night. It is thought that these animals disperse to different habitats or find mates by swimming when visual predators find it hard to see them. In some cases only one sex will emerge at night, and often that sex is morphologically better suited for swimming.

Horizontal migrations of fish that span distances of hundreds of metres to tens of kilometres are common and generally related to patterns of feeding or reproduction. Tropical coral trout (*Plectropomus* species) remain dispersed over a reef for most of the year, but adults will aggregate at certain locations at the time of spawning. Transoceanic migrations (greater than 1,000 km [about 620 miles]) are observed in a number of marine vertebrates, and these movements often relate to requirements of feeding and reproduction. Bluefin tuna (*Thunnus*

Atlantic salmon migrate from salt water to fresh when they spawn, swimming against river currents and obstacles such as waterfalls in the process.
Keith Ringland/Photolibrary/Getty Images

thynnus) traverse the Atlantic Ocean in a single year; they spawn in the Caribbean, then swim to high latitudes of the Atlantic to feed on the rich supply of fish. Turtles and sharks also migrate great distances.

Fish that spend their lives in both marine and freshwater systems (diadromous animals) exhibit some of the most spectacular migratory behaviour. Anadromous fishes (those that spend most of their lives in the sea but migrate to fresh water to spawn) such as Atlantic salmon (*Salmo salar*) also have unique migratory patterns. After spawning, the adults die. Newly hatched fish (alevin) emerge from spawned eggs and develop into young fry that move down rivers toward the sea. Juveniles (parr) grow into larger fish (smolt) that convene near the ocean. When the adult fish are ready to spawn, they return to the river in which they were born (natal river), using a variety of environmental cues, including the Earth's magnetic field, the Sun, and water chemistry. It is believed that the thyroid gland has a role in imprinting the water chemistry of the natal river on the fish. Freshwater eels such as the European eel (*Anguilla anguilla*) undertake great migrations from fresh water to spawn in the marine waters of the Sargasso Sea (catadromous migrations), where they die. Eel larvae, called leptocephalus larvae, drift back to Europe in the Gulf Stream.

THE DYNAMICS OF POPULATIONS AND SPECIES ASSEMBLAGES IN MARINE ECOSYSTEMS

A wide variety of processes influence the dynamics of marine populations of individual species and the composition of assemblages (e.g., collections of populations of different species that live in the same area). With the exception of marine mammals such as whales, fish that bear live young (e.g., embiotocid fish), and brooders (i.e., fauna that incubate their offspring until they emerge as larvae or juveniles), most marine organisms produce a large number of offspring of which few survive. Processes that affect the plankton can have a great influence on the numbers of young that survive to be recruited, or relocated, into adult populations. The survival of larvae may depend on the abundance of food at various times and in various places, the number of predators, and oceanographic features that retain larvae near suitable nursery areas. The number of organisms recruited to benthic and pelagic systems may ultimately determine the size of adult populations and therefore the relative abundance of species in marine assemblages. However, many processes can affect the survival of organisms after recruitment. Predators eat recruits, and mortality rates in prey species can vary with time and space, thus changing original population patterns established in recruitment.

Patterns of colonization and succession can have a significant impact on benthic assemblages. For example, when intertidal reefs are cleared experimentally, the assemblage of organisms that colonize the bare space often reflects the types of larvae available in local waters at the time. Tube worms may dominate if they establish themselves first; if they fail to do so, algal spores may colonize the shore first and inhibit the settlement of these worms. Competition between organisms may also play a role. Long-term data gathered over periods of more than 25 years from coral reefs have demonstrated that some corals (e.g., *Acropora cytherea*) competitively overgrow neighbouring corals. Physical disturbance from hurricanes destroys many corals, and during regrowth competitively inferior species can coexist with normally dominant species on the reef. Chemical defenses of sessile organisms also can deter the growth or cause increased mortality of organisms that settle on them. Ascidian larvae (e.g.,

Podoclavella) often avoid settling on sponges (e.g., *Mycale*); when this does occur, the larvae rarely reach adulthood.

Although the processes that determine species assemblages may be understood, variations occur in the composition of the plankton that make it difficult to predict patterns of colonization with great accuracy.

BIOLOGICAL PRODUCTIVITY

Primary productivity is the rate at which energy is converted by photosynthetic and chemosynthetic autotrophs to organic substances. The total amount of productivity in a region or system is gross primary productivity. A certain amount of organic material is used to sustain the life of producers; what remains is net productivity. Net marine primary productivity is the amount of organic material available to support the consumers (herbivores and carnivores) of the sea. The standing crop is the total biomass (weight) of vegetation. Most primary productivity is carried out by pelagic phytoplankton, not benthic plants.

Most primary producers require nitrogen and phosphorus, which are available in the ocean as nitrate, nitrite, ammonia, and phosphorus. The abundances of these molecules and the intensity and quality of light exert a major influence on rates of production. The two principal categories of producers (autotrophs) in the sea are pelagic phytoplankton and benthic microalgae and macroalgae. Benthic plants grow only on the fringe of the world's oceans and are estimated to produce only 5 to 10 percent of the total marine plant material in a year. Chemoautotrophs are the producers of the deep-sea vents.

Primary productivity is usually determined by measuring the uptake of carbon dioxide or the output of oxygen. Production rates are usually expressed as grams of organic carbon per unit area per unit time. The productivity of the entire ocean is estimated to be approximately 16×10^{10} tons of carbon per year, which is about eight times that of the land.

THE PELAGIC FOOD CHAIN

Food chains in coastal waters of the world are generally regulated by nutrient concentrations. These concentrations determine the abundance of phytoplankton, which in turn provide food for the primary consumers, such as protozoa and zooplankton, that the higher-level consumers—fish, squid, and marine mammals—prey upon. It had been thought that phytoplankton in the 5- to 100-micrometre size range were responsible for most of the primary production in the sea and that grazers such as copepods controlled the numbers of phytoplankton. Data gathered since 1975, however, indicate that the system is much more complex than this.

It is now thought that most primary production in marine waters of the world is accomplished by single-celled 0.5- to 10-micrometre phototrophs (bacteria and protists). Moreover, heterotrophic protists (phagotrophic protists) are now viewed as the dominant controllers of both bacteria and primary production in the sea. Current models of pelagic marine food chains picture complex interactions within a microbial food web. Larger metazoans are supported by the production of autotrophic and heterotrophic cells.

UPWELLING

The most productive waters of the world are in regions of upwelling. In coastal waters, upwelling brings nutrients toward the surface. Phytoplankton reproduce rapidly in these conditions, and grazing zooplankton also multiply and provide abundant food supplies for nekton. Some of the world's richest fisheries are found in regions of upwelling—for example, the temperate waters off Peru and California. If upwelling fails, the effects on animals that depend on it can be disastrous. Fisheries also suffer at these times, as evidenced by the collapse of the Peruvian anchovy industry in the 1970s. The intensity and location of upwelling are influenced by changes in atmospheric circulation, as exemplified by the influence of El Niño conditions.

SEASONAL CYCLES OF PRODUCTION

Cycles of plankton production vary at different latitudes because seasonal patterns of light and temperature vary dramatically with latitude. In the extreme conditions at the poles, plankton populations crash during the constant darkness of winter and bloom in summer with long hours of light and the retreat of the ice field. In tropical waters, variation in sunlight and temperature is slight, nutrients are present in low concentrations, and planktonic assemblages do not undergo large fluctuations in abundance. There are, however, rapid cycles of reproduction and high rates of grazing and predation that result in a rapid turnover of plankton and a low standing crop. In temperate regions plankton abundance peaks in spring as temperature and the length and intensity of daylight increase. Moreover, seasonal winter storms usually mix the water column, creating a more even distribution of the nutrients, which facilitates the growth of phytoplankton. Peak zooplankton production generally lags behind that of phytoplankton, while the consumption of phytoplankton by zooplankton and phagotrophic protists is thought to reduce phytoplankton abundance. Secondary peaks in abundance occur in autumn.

Seasonal peaks of some plankton are very conspicuous, and the composition of the plankton varies considerably. In spring and early summer many fish and invertebrates spawn and release eggs and larvae into the plankton, and, as a result, the meroplanktonic component of the plankton is higher at these times. General patterns of plankton abundance may be further influenced by local conditions. Heavy rainfall in coastal regions (especially areas in which monsoons prevail) can result in nutrient-rich turbid plumes (i.e., estuarine or riverine plumes) that extend into waters of the continental shelf. Changes in production, therefore, may depend on the season, the proximity to fresh water, and the timing and location of upwelling, currents, and patterns of reproduction.

RIVERINE AND LACUSTRINE ECOSYSTEMS

Although riverine and lacustrine ecosystems (also known as lotic and lentic ecosystems) are aquatic, they differ significantly from marine ecosystems. Riverine ecosystems are characterized by flowing waters, whereas lacustrine ecosystems are those that occur in still waters.

Riverine ecosystems can be described as any spring, stream, or river viewed as an ecosystem. The waters are flowing and exhibit a longitudinal gradation in temperatures, concentration of dissolved material, turbidity, and atmospheric gases, from the source to the mouth. There are two major zones: rapids, shallow water where currents are strong enough to keep the bottom clear and firm; and pools, deeper waters where currents are reduced and silt and other debris collect on the bottom. Each zone has its specially adapted life-forms.

In contrast, lacustrine ecosystems occur in ponds and lakes. Ponds are relatively shallow, with considerable light penetration. They support a variety of rooted aquatic plants. Water is mixed well top to bottom, but there are great seasonal changes in wind, temperature, precipitation, and evaporation. It is a precarious habitat subject to much imbalance, and the animal inhabitants must possess considerable physiological adaptability to survive. Lakes, on the other hand, are larger and deeper, often stratified in terms of light penetration, temperature range, and oxygen concentration. Such gradations from top to bottom profoundly affect the life of lakes in terms of distribution and adaptation. Seasonal changes are gradual and include spring and fall overturns of water and summer and winter stratification.

Three major zones of habitat are usually present in lacustrine ecosystems:

1. littoral, the shallow-water zone, with light penetrating to the bottom and supporting rooted plants and bottom-dwelling animals
2. limnetic, the water open to effective light penetration, supporting plant and animal plankton
3. profundal, the bottom and deepwater area beyond light penetration, supporting dark-adapted organisms.

THE BOUNDARY ECOSYSTEM

Boundary ecosystems are complexes of living organisms in areas where one body of water meets another, e.g., estuaries and lagoons, or where a body of water meets the land, e.g., marshes. The latter are often called wetlands.

Boundary ecosystems are characterized by the presence of large plants. In the open water of the ocean and large lakes the basic production of living material (primary production) is carried out by microscopic algae (phytoplankton) floating freely in the water. At the bottom there is not enough light to allow growth of large, attached plants. In boundary ecosystems much of the area is shallow enough for light to reach the bottom and permit large plants to grow. Phytoplankton is also present, but the large plants give the boundary systems their special character.

Boundary Systems Between Waters

Boundary systems include estuaries and lagoons. Estuaries are places where rivers meet the sea and may be defined as areas where salt water is measurably diluted with fresh water. Lagoons are bodies of water partially or completely separated from the open ocean by barriers of sand or coral.

Estuaries

On average, estuaries are biologically more productive than either the adjacent river or the sea because they have a special kind of water circulation that traps plant nutrients and stimulates primary production. Fresh water, being lighter than salt water, tends to form a distinct layer that floats at the surface of the estuary. At the boundary between fresh and salt water, there is a certain amount of mixing caused by the flow of fresh water over salt and by the ebb and flow of tides. Additional mixing may be caused from time to time by strong winds and by internal waves that are propagated along the interface between fresh and salt water. Four types of estuary are recognized according to the degree of mixing: salt wedge estuaries, partially mixed estuaries, vertically homogeneous estuaries, and fjords.

A salt wedge estuary has minimal mixing and the salt water forms a wedge, thickest at the seaward end, tapering to a very thin layer at the landward limit. The penetration of this wedge changes with the flow of the river. During flood conditions the wedge will retreat; during low flows it will extend farther upriver. The mouth of the Mississippi

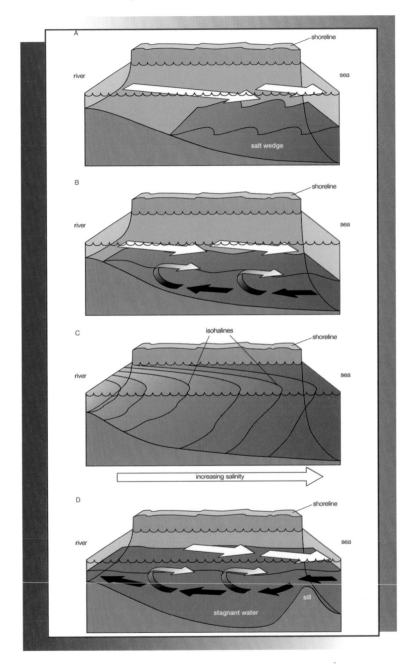

Four main types of estuaries: (A) salt wedge estuary, (B) partially mixed estuary, (C) vertically homogeneous estuary, and (D) fjord. (Black arrows indicate saltwater and white arrows, fresh water.) Encyclopædia Britannica, Inc.

River in the United States is a classic example. The mixing at the boundary between fresh and salt water causes the surface layer to entrain salt water and become more saline as it moves toward the sea. To compensate for the entrained salt water there is a slow movement of the salt water up the estuary at depth. Because bottom waters are rich in nutrients derived from decomposing plant and animal remains, this circulation has the effect of pumping nutrients into the estuary and stimulating biological production.

Organic and inorganic particles carried by rivers tend to flocculate (aggregate into a mass) and sediment out when they encounter salt water. They sink from the freshwater layer to the salt wedge and are carried upstream. When the organic matter decomposes, it adds still more nutrients to the estuary. The inorganic matter settles on the bottom and provides an enriched sediment for flowering plants adapted to salt water. Between the tide marks, mangrove forests flourish in tropical conditions, while salt marshes form in temperate and subarctic conditions. Below low tide, sea grasses form dense beds on muddy substrates. In areas of an estuary where water movement is vigorous enough to remove sediment, leaving a stony or rocky bottom, rooted plants are replaced by seaweeds. These have a special structure known as a holdfast, which attaches itself to any hard surface. Phytoplankton floating freely in the water benefits from the high level of nutrients, especially near the head of the estuary, and grows rapidly. It provides food for the microscopic animals in the water column, the zooplankton. As this community is carried downstream in the surface waters, dead organisms and the fecal pellets of the animals sink toward the bottom and enter the salt wedge to be carried back to the head of the estuary. As they decompose they add still more nutrients to the water.

In a partially mixed estuary, the vigorous rise and fall of the tide generates strong turbulence and causes partial mixing between the fresh water above and the salt water below. Under these conditions the river flow entrains 10 to 20 or more times its own volume of salt water, and the compensatory landward flow of seawater near the bottom is correspondingly increased. The effect of the Earth's rotation (Coriolis effect) is to cause the surface flow to be stronger on the right-hand side facing seaward, or the opposite in the Southern Hemisphere. The bottom flow is stronger on the opposite side of the estuary.

In a vertically homogeneous estuary the river flow is weak and the tidal flow is strong. Consequently, all stratification is broken down and salinity is almost the same from top to bottom at any given place. The salinity is lowest where the river enters the estuary and highest near the sea.

The fjord-type estuary was originally formed by a glacier and has a submerged ridge, or sill, near its mouth, composed of glacial deposits. It may be regarded as a partially mixed estuary in which the bottom has been replaced by a basin of undiluted seawater held in place by the sill. When entrainment in river flow causes a strong landward flow at the bottom, water rises over the sill and enters the estuary at intermediate depth, leaving the deep waters undisturbed. Only major intrusions of seawater caused by storms can displace the deep water. Owing to their glacial origin, fjords commonly have steep sides and very little shallow water. Hence, the development of salt marshes or sea-grass beds is minimal, but seaweeds colonize the rocky shores.

The high level of plant production in estuaries supports a correspondingly high level of production of invertebrate animals and fish. Estuaries often contain beds of shellfish such as mussels and oysters and large populations of shrimps and crabs. Fish such as plaice and flounders are common. Other species use the estuaries as nursery grounds. Organisms in early stages of development enter the salt wedge at the seaward end and are carried up the estuary by the bottom currents. Juveniles find abundant food as well as protection from predators in the mangrove forests, salt marshes, or sea-grass beds that line the estuary. Later, they may migrate to the open ocean to continue their growth and development. Other species pass through the estuaries in the course of their migrations. For example, salmon migrate from the sea to the rivers to spawn, while the young fish later migrate back to the sea. Eels migrate in the opposite direction, breeding in the sea but returning to fresh water as juveniles.

Many estuaries are now important sites for aquaculture. There is a long history of mussel culture along the coast of Spain, and Norwegian fjords are much used for salmon culture. In Southeast Asia, artificial ponds are created in mangrove forests and used to culture shrimp. Because estuaries are located at the mouths of rivers, they have been favoured sites for the development of human settlements. This has made them particularly vulnerable to contamination by sewage and industrial effluents. The characteristic circulation that serves to trap natural plant nutrients may also retain high concentrations of pollutants.

LAGOONS

In coastal lagoons the barrier most often is formed and reinforced by the movement of sand in alongshore currents. Coral lagoons occupy the space between a coral reef and the shore or within the central basin of a coral atoll. Lagoons are characteristically shallow, and, with an abundance of large plants, they are highly productive.

The circulation of water in a coastal lagoon is very dependent on the amount of land drainage. A lagoon into

AQUACULTURE

Aquaculture, which is also known as fish farming, fish culture, or mariculture, is the approximate equivalent in fishing to agriculture—that is, the rearing of fish, shellfish, and some aquatic plants to supplement the natural supply. Fish are reared under controlled conditions all over the world.

Fish may be confined in earth ponds, concrete pools, barricaded coastal waters, or cages suspended in open water. In these enclosures, the fish can be supplied with adequate food and protected from many natural predators.

While most fish farming is devoted to the commercial food market, many governmental agencies engage in it to stock lakes and rivers for sport fishing; there is, in addition, a steady commercial market for goldfish and other decorative fish for home aquariums. Aquaculturists also raise bait fish for both sport and commercial fishing.

Ocean ranching by governments is intended to restock lakes and oceans. The young fish are bred in the controlled environment and when sufficiently mature are released into the open sea. Oysters (as a source of both food and pearls), scallops, and mussels are raised throughout most of the world. Carp, trout, catfish, and tilapia are also widely raised. Experiments with ocean ranching in the late 20th century led to the economically successful aquaculture of lobsters.

which a major river flows is known as an estuarine lagoon and may be regarded as a special kind of estuary. There are, however, many cases in hot arid regions in which lagoons lose more water by evaporation than they receive from land drainage. This causes surface waters to become more dense than seawater and to sink to the bottom. Seawater flows in at the surface to replace that lost by evaporation, creating a circulation the reverse of that found in estuaries. If exchange with the open sea is limited, the lagoon may become much more saline than the open sea. Consequently, various species of plants and animals have become adapted to life in high salinities.

WETLANDS

Wetlands generally occur at the interface between terrestrial ecosystems, such as upland forests and grasslands, and aquatic ecosystems, such as rivers, deep lakes, and oceans. Thus, wetlands are neither wholly terrestrial nor wholly aquatic but exhibit characteristics of each. They also depend greatly on both. Because wetlands occur at the interface of a body of water and the land, they are examples of boundary ecosystems.

Wetlands are characterized by poor drainage and the consequent presence most or all of the time of sluggishly moving or standing water saturating the soil. Wetlands are usually classified, according to soil and plant life, as bog, marsh, or swamp.

Bogs

A bog is a type of wetland ecosystem characterized by wet, spongy, poorly drained peaty soil. Bogs can be divided into three types: (1) typical bogs of cool regions, dominated by the growth of bog mosses, *Sphagnum,* and heaths, particularly *Chamaedaphne* (northern bogs with trees growing on them are often called muskegs); (2) fens, dominated by grasslike plants, grasses, sedges, and reeds; and (3) tropical tree bogs, in which the peat may be formed almost entirely from tree remains. Typical, or *Sphagnum,* bogs are highly acid with a pH (index of acidity–alkalinity) of less than five (seven being neutral) and are associated with waters containing no more minerals than are contained in rainwater, often the only source of water for a bog. Fens are watered with groundwater that has some dissolved minerals and that has a pH above five; that is, it is only moderately acid. Fens and bogs are often associated in one area that usually is called a bog. Tropical bogs occur only in areas where the water is very low in minerals. They are less common than swamps but still cover extensive areas in Malaya, Indonesia, tropical South America, and Africa.

The saturation of the moss with water retards passage of air, so that parts of a mass of *Sphagnum* more than a few inches from the surface are usually anoxic. The combination of lack of oxygen, lack of minerals, and highly acid condition greatly retards the action of bacteria and fungi, the usual decay organisms. With the retardation of decomposition of the dead moss, a *Sphagnum* peat develops under the living plants. This is particularly the case in areas where there is a mean annual temperature of below 10° C (50° F), which also retards decay.

Bogs are most common in parts of the world that were glaciated during the Pleistocene Epoch (2,600,000 to 11,700 years ago). They cover vast areas in the tundra and

A bog of Connemara, a peninsula between a harbour and a bay in Galway, Ireland. Bogs are abundant in the British Isles because of the area's climate—cooler temperatures with copious rainfall. Travel Ink/Gallo Images/ Getty Images

boreal forest regions of Canada, northern Europe, and Russia. Areas of high rainfall farther to the south, such as the wetter parts of the British Isles, also contain extensive bogs. Glacial ice created many local depressions by scouring underlying rocks and spreading an uneven deposit of till on the ground. With the melting of the ice, these depressions filled with water. If the mineral content of the water was low, the ponds so formed were colonized by *Sphagnum,* which converted them to bogs.

Once bogs are formed, they retard the development of efficient drainage by inhibiting water movement and slowing erosion of the soil or rocks on which they rest. Thus, bogs tend to be long-lived if temperatures remain low and sufficient excess of rainfall over evaporation exists to prevent their drying out. If they do dry out, upland plants will colonize the former bog.

The peat underlying a *Sphagnum* bog is composed largely of partly decomposed moss. There may be some inclusion of windblown particles, pollen, and dust. The water content of peat may be as high as 90 percent. The ash content of dried peat varies from 2 to 20 percent, with lower values more usual because the higher ash amounts come from sand and clay blown into the peat when it was at the surface. Other chemical characteristics of peat underlying bogs are the absence of free oxygen; the presence of carbon dioxide at high pressure, though in small amounts; low electrolyte concentration; and high acidity.

In general, temperatures in lowland tropical areas are high enough for organic decay to be too fast for large quantities of peat to accumulate. But in areas with very high rainfall and with groundwater of very low mineral content, bogs may occur. As is the case in colder regions, the bogs may fill low basins, or they may develop into raised bogs.

MARSHES

Marshes are a type of wetland ecosystem characterized by poorly drained mineral soils and by plant life dominated by grasses. The latter characteristic distinguishes a marsh from a swamp, whose plant life is dominated by trees.

Marshes are common at the mouths of rivers, especially where extensive deltas have been built. The river brings a steady supply of water. The gradient of the river approaches zero at the sea, where flow is sluggish. Because the delta is deposited by sediment settling from the river water, the land that is built will be poorly drained at its driest and will often be under water. Sediment supplied by the river has often been eroded from the surface soils of the drainage basin and is thus very rich. The combination of water supplied steadily at a low rate over a waterlogged but rich soil creates a perfect environment for marsh grasses.

Fibrous-rooted grasses bind the muds together and further hinder water flow, thus encouraging the spread of both the delta and the marsh. Marshes occur in the deltas of most of the world's great rivers. In Europe well-known river-mouth marshes include those of the Camargue in the Rhône Delta, the Guadalquivir in Spain, and the Danube in Romania, all of which are famous as bird sanctuaries. In the Middle East, both the Nile Delta and the delta of the Tigris–Euphrates have extensive marshes of historical importance. The marsh dwellers of the Iranian marshes have developed a unique culture adapted to life in the wetlands. Marshes occur in the deltas of the Mekong in Vietnam and the Amazon in Brazil. In the United States, the most extensive delta marshes are those of the Mississippi River.

Some low-lying areas with poor drainage at the heads of more extensive drainage patterns contain wetlands. A well-known example is the Pripet Marshes and fens that historically have served as the natural boundary between Poland and Russia. In some places basin-like depressions in the Earth's surface trap waters and make wetlands. Most such areas are drained someplace along their rim by a river that is impeded at that point sufficiently to dam water at times of high flow and create marshes and swamps. The world's two largest rivers, the Amazon and the Congo, fall into this category. Both of the great basins named after these rivers have extensive wetlands. The papyrus marshes of the upper Nile in southern Sudan lie above dams of resistant rocks of the cataracts.

The Okavango Marshes east of the Kalahari desert in Botswana are perhaps the best example of marshes formed in an interior, closed basin that has no drainage. Other

Sawgrass is the dominant plant life in the Everglades, a marsh area that covers some 4,300 square miles (11,100 square km) of southern Florida in the United States. Shutterstock.com

basins without outlets like that of the Great Salt Lake in Utah have accumulated too much salt for marsh growth.

The Florida Everglades constitutes a unique marsh–swamp combination growing on a limestone base. Because the region is near sea level the water from the abundant rains does not drain but remains on the surface. The Everglades is similar to a huge, shallow, slowly flowing river. The area is an ideal marsh habitat but the Everglades is different from usual marshes. The soils are alkaline because of the limy base, and the water is clear.

Some areas, such as the northern Great Plains of the United States, have so many small marshes that they are a characteristic of the landscape. These small marshes formed because the landscape left by the retreat of glacial ice was so irregular and so poorly drained that countless little depressions were filled with water each spring. As snow melted, the depressions supported the growth of temporary marshes, which then dried up during the summer. Larger depressions were occupied by ponds. These gradually became marshy as they filled in with sediment.

Salt marshes, which are extensive along the east coast of the United States and are also common in the Arctic, northern Europe, Australia, and New Zealand, are formed by seawater flooding and draining, which exposes flat areas of intertidal land. Salt-marsh grasses will not grow on permanently flooded flats; growth is also prevented where the flooded land is subject to strong currents and is therefore unstable.

Animals have adapted to the limited supplies of oxygen in salt-marsh water in various ways. Rat-tailed maggots (*Tubifera*), for example, survive in shallow marshes by means of a telescoping, tail-breathing tube that they extend to the water surface for air. Some larvae of shore flies (Ephydridae) and some nematodes take advantage of the air spaces in plants and obtain oxygen from that source.

Many small marsh animals have great resistance to lack of oxygen; for example, many nematodes can live indefinitely in the complete absence of oxygen. This ability is essential for such minute animals that would otherwise be limited in distribution to a thin layer a fraction of an inch deep at the mud surface.

Salt-marsh animals living at or in the ground are largely derived from marine ancestors and have a problem in resisting fresh water from rains rather than salt. Some, such as worms, merely hide in the mud until the freshwater has run off the marsh surface. Others, such as fiddler crabs, have developed the ability to control their osmotic concentration in freshwater for periods of up to several days. Insects are the principal land animals found on marshes. Although they can withstand short periods of saltwater immersion, they often avoid saltwater by moving up the plants or flying away.

Salt marshes are among the most productive natural systems. Productivities of more than 3,000 grams per square metre per year have been reported for the most productive parts of salt marshes, the tall *Spartina alterniflora* stands growing along tidal creeks. These values correspond to nearly 30 tons per acre per year and are equal to the highest values that have been achieved in agriculture.

Swamps

Swamps are characterized by mineral soils with poor drainage and by plant life dominated by trees. The latter characteristic distinguishes a swamp from a marsh, in which plant life consists largely of grasses. Swamps are found throughout the world. They exist in areas with poor drainage and sufficient water supply to keep the ground waterlogged, and they have a high enough supply of minerals in the water to stimulate decay of organisms and prevent the accumulation of organic materials. They are often found in regions of low relief associated with rivers that supply the water. Compare marsh.

Rivers in mature valleys frequently have extensive marshes and swamps along their sides. Floodplains elevated only a few feet above river level, abandoned river channels, and oxbows may have standing or sluggishly flowing water for appreciable parts of the year and thus support swamps and marshes.

River swamps are abundant along the coastal plain in the southeastern United States. They are delightfully described in their primeval condition by William Bartram in his account *Travels Through North and South Carolina, Georgia, East and West Florida*, written in 1791. These were the swamps that Francis Marion used so successfully to escape the British forces during the Revolutionary War and the source of his nickname, "the old swamp fox."

The Great Dismal Swamp, of North Carolina and Virginia, actually a mixture of waterways, swamps, and marshes, is a coastal-plain swamp, although it is not associated with a large river. The Mississippi and its lower tributaries, such as the Red River and parallel rivers in eastern Texas, have extensive swamps along the sluggish portions that flow through the coastal plain. The Paraná and Paraguay rivers in South America have extensive swamps and marshes along their courses. A mixture of swamps and marshes in Georgia called the Okefenokee Swamp is the source of the Suwannee River. As a unique marsh-swamp combination, the Florida Everglades contain large cypress swamps, mostly in the wetlands' northwest.

Topography and water supply are the two most important features in determining the distribution of freshwater swamps. The nature of soils and bedrock is of importance in determining the drainage in a region, but wetlands may exist locally on any base from sands to impervious rock.

The flow of water through wetlands is slow because of low gradients and retarding effects of the vegetation. Dead plant matter settles rather than being washed away. The slow replacement and lack of turbulence in the water result in a low rate of oxygen supply. Decay of the dead vegetation quickly uses up what oxygen is supplied, so that the mud and bottom waters are low or lacking in oxygen content. Under these conditions, the decay of organic matter is incomplete. This causes an accumulation of the more resistant fraction (humates and tannins) in the substratum. The familiar swamp water, varying from yellow to such a deep brown that it resembles strong tea or coffee, is the result.

Extensive swamps develop mainly where land runoff is sufficient to bring a supply of sediments that accumulate and extend the swamp. The deltas of the Mekong, Amazon, Congo, and Ganges and the north coast of Australia and of Sumatra have notable and extensive mangrove swamps.

FUNCTIONS AND VALUES OF WETLANDS

Wetland functions are physical, chemical, and biological processes or attributes that are vital to the integrity of the wetland system. Because wetlands are often transition zones (ecotones) between uplands and deepwater aquatic systems, many processes that take place in them have a global impact: they can affect the export of organic materials or serve as a sink for inorganic nutrients. This intermediary position is also responsible for the biodiversity often encountered in these regions, as wetlands "borrow" species from nearby aquatic and terrestrial systems.

Wetlands play a major role in the biosphere by providing habitats for a great abundance and richness of floral and faunal species; they are also the last havens for many rare and endangered species. Some wetlands are considered among the Earth's most productive ecosystems. The wetland's function as a site of biodiversity is also valuable to humans, who rely on these ecosystems for commercial and sport fishing, hunting, and recreational uses. The capacity of wetlands to absorb a great amount of water also benefits developed areas. A wetland system can protect shorelines, cleanse polluted waters, prevent floods, and recharge groundwater aquifers, earning wetlands the sobriquet "the kidneys of the landscape."

CONCLUSION

Throughout geologic time, Earth's biosphere has been a dynamic region of the planet. From its humble beginnings in shallow ocean, Earth's life zone has expanded as living things diversified and became more sophisticated. Today, life covers the surface of most of Earth's landmasses and fills the productive regions of the oceans. The hardiest life-forms exist in or near hydrothermal vents in the oceans or other extreme environments.

As many of Earth's life-forms have become more complex, Earth's biosphere has also increased in complexity. Individual ecosystems filled with organisms range from those that exist at tiny scales, such as in single drops of water, to the largest scales, such as those that span large portions of continents. (The largest ecosystems contain multitudes of smaller, nested ecosystems.) All are self-regulating, cycling nutrients between the ecosystem's living and nonliving components and transferring energy from primary producing organisms to consuming organisms.

At larger scales, the planet can be divided into several plant kingdoms and animal realms. All of these regions were molded by plate tectonics and continental arrangement, the movement of warm and cold ocean currents, changes in climate across geologic time, and by the organisms themselves. Volcanoes, floods, earthquakes, ice sheets, and other phenomena continually modify Earth's surface. These forces destroy and fragment ecosystems, forcing the hardiest organisms to adapt to the new conditions and bringing about new arrangements of interacting organisms as well as the resources that support them.

Life on Earth is, thus far, a miracle in the universe. The planet's tremendous biodiversity is a wonder to behold. However, many of Earth's species face the threat of extinction. In the past, extraterrestrial impacts, volcanism, and the resulting climatic changes caused huge numbers of species to pass away. Today, many of Earth's ecosystems and much of its biodiversity are threatened by human beings. As the human population increases, more and more of Earth's resources—which had been used previously to support other organisms—are allocated to food production, building construction, energy for heating and transportation, road development, and other activities. As a result, new urbanized ecosystems have arisen in many areas around the globe. Some species have adapted to these new ecological structures, but many more have not. Time will tell whether humans can limit the damage caused by their own success.

APPENDIX: SIGNIFICANT ECOSYSTEM COMPONENTS AND CONCEPTS

BACTERIA AND FUNGI

Bacteria and fungi found in water belong by definition to plankton community, but, because of special techniques required for sampling and identification, they usually are considered separately. These organisms are important in the transformation of dead organic materials to inorganic plant nutrients. Some of these marine and freshwater microorganisms (including blue-green algae) fix molecular nitrogen from water containing dissolved air, forming ammonia or related nutrients important for phytoplankton growth. Although little is known about the extent of nitrogen fixation, bacteria and fungi always are found in water samples. A peculiar situation exists in the Black Sea, where water below 130–180 metres contains hydrogen sulfide and no oxygen. Under these conditions only bacteria are found.

BENTHOS

Benthos is the name for the assemblage of organisms inhabiting the seafloor. Benthic epifauna live upon the seafloor or upon bottom objects; the so-called infauna live within the sediments of the seafloor. By far the best-studied benthos are the macrobenthos, those forms larger than 1 mm (0.04 inch), which are dominated by polychaete worms, pelecypods, anthozoans, echinoderms, sponges, ascidians, and crustaceans. Meiobenthos, those organisms between

0.1 and 1 mm in size, include polychaetes, pelecypods, copepods, ostracodes, cumaceans, nematodes, turbellarians, and foraminiferans. The microbenthos, smaller than 0.1 mm, include bacteria, diatoms, ciliates, amoeba, and flagellates.

The variety and abundance of the benthos vary with latitude, depth, water temperature and salinity, locally determined conditions such as the nature of the substrate, and ecological circumstances such as predation and competition. The principal food sources for the benthos are plankton and organic debris from land. In shallow water, larger algae are important, and, where light reaches the bottom, benthic photosynthesizing diatoms are also a significant food source. Hard and sandy substrates are populated by suspension feeders such as sponges and pelecypods. Softer bottoms are dominated by deposit eaters, of which the polychaetes are the most important. Fishes, starfish, snails, cephalopods, and the larger crustaceans are important predators and scavengers.

BIOMASS

Biomass is equivalent to the weight or total quantity of living organisms of one animal or plant species (species biomass) or of all the species in the community (community biomass). It is commonly referred to a unit area or volume of habitat. The weight or quantity of organisms in an area at a given moment is the standing crop. The total amount of organic material produced by living organisms of a particular area within a set period of time, called the primary or secondary productivity (the former for plants, the latter for animals), is usually measured in units of energy, such as gram calories or kilojoules per square metre per year. Measures of weight—e.g., tons of carbon per square kilometre per year—are also commonly recorded.

In a different though related sense, the term *biomass* refers to plant materials and animal waste used especially as a source of fuel.

DETRITUS

In ecology, detritus is matter composed of leaves and other plant parts, animal remains, waste products, and other organic debris that falls onto the soil or into bodies of water from surrounding terrestrial communities. Microorganisms (such as bacteria or fungi) break down detritus, and this microorganism-rich material is eaten by invertebrates, which are in turn eaten by vertebrates. Many freshwater streams have detritus rather than living plants as their energy base.

FOOD CHAINS

A food chain is a sequence of transfers of matter and energy from organism to organism in the form of food. Food chains intertwine locally into a food web because most organisms consume more than one type of animal or plant. Plants, which convert solar energy to food by photosynthesis, are the primary food source. In a predator chain, a plant-eating animal is eaten by a flesh-eating animal. In a parasite chain, a smaller organism consumes part of a larger host and may itself be parasitized by even smaller organisms. In a saprophytic chain, microorganisms live on dead organic matter.

Because energy, in the form of heat, is lost at each step, or trophic level, chains do not normally encompass more than four or five trophic levels. People can increase the total food supply by cutting out one step in the food chain: instead of consuming animals that eat cereal grains, the people themselves consume the grains. Because the food chain is made shorter, the total amount of energy available to the final consumers is increased.

HERBIVORES

Herbivores are animals adapted to subsist solely on plant tissues. A number of herbivores have the ability to digest cellulose, the basic component in the cell walls of plant cells. The herbivores range from insects (such as aphids) to large mammals (such as elephants).

OMNIVORES

Omnivores are animals with wide food preferences, which can eat both plant and animal matter. Many small birds and mammals are omnivorous; deer mice and mockingbirds have diets that at different times may include a preponderance of insects or berries. Many animals generally considered carnivores are actually omnivorous, among them the red fox, which enjoys fruits and berries, and the snapping turtle, one-third of whose diet is provided by plants.

LITTORAL ZONE

The littoral zone is the marine ecological realm that experiences the effects of tidal and longshore currents and breaking waves to a depth of 5 to 10 metres (16 to 33 feet) below the low-tide level, depending on the intensity of storm waves. The zone is characterized by abundant dissolved oxygen, sunlight, nutrients, generally high wave energies and water motion, and, in the intertidal subzone, alternating submergence and exposure. The geological nature of shorelines and nearshore bottoms is exceedingly varied. Consequently, the littoral fauna taken as a whole involves an enormous number of species and every major phylum, although the number of individuals may vary widely with locality. Coral reefs, rocky coasts, sandy beaches, and sheltered embayments each possess specialized, intricately interrelated floral and faunal littoral populations.

The types of living things that inhabit a littoral zone depend to a considerable extent on the type of bottom and on the degree of the zone's exposure to wave action. Exposed sandy coasts generally develop sparse populations, especially between the tide lines, while the few organisms inhabiting wave-swept rocky shores are generally firmly cemented or anchored to the substratum. Bays and inlets that are protected from violent wave action often develop rich populations, however. Protected rocky shores are generally covered with seaweeds, mussels, barnacles, and so on, with various kinds of crabs and worms crawling among them. Protected sandy and muddy bottoms teem with burrowing mollusks, worms, and echinoderms.

MACROFAUNA

In soil science, macrofauna includes all animals that are one centimetre (0.4 inch) or more long but smaller than an earthworm. Potworms, myriapods, centipedes, millipedes, slugs, snails, fly larvae, beetles, beetle larvae, and spiders are typical members of the macrofauna. Many of these animals burrow in the soil, aiding soil drainage and aeration; in addition, some organic material passes into the soil through the burrows. Most macrofauna consume decaying plant material and organic debris, but centipedes, some insects, and spiders prey on other soil animals.

MEGAFAUNA

In soil science, megafauna includes animals such as earthworms and small vertebrates (e.g., moles, mice, hares, rabbits, gophers, snakes, and lizards). The food habits of soil megafauna vary; earthworms ingest both soil and organic matter, but most of the vertebrates feed on plant material, invertebrates, and other small vertebrate animals. Megafauna are the principal agents of soil turnover and distribution; this movement loosens soil structure, improves aeration and drainage, and distributes soil microorganisms.

Outside of soil science, the term *megafauna* refers to the largest mammals (and sometimes the largest birds and reptiles), often those that were the first to be exterminated following human contact.

MESOFAUNA

Mesofauna (or Meiofauna) in soil science includes intermediate-sized animals (those greater than 40 microns in length, which is about three times the thickness of a human hair). Nematodes, mites, springtails, proturans, and pauropods are typical members of the mesofauna. These animals may feed upon microorganisms, other soil animals, decaying plant or animal material, living plants, or fungi. Most mesofauna feed on decaying plant material; by removing roots they open drainage and aeration channels in the soil. The channels contain mesofaunal fecal material that can be broken down by smaller organisms.

MICROFAUNA

Microfauna is the designation for small, often microscopic animals, especially those inhabiting the soil, an organ, or other localized habitat. Single-celled protozoans, small nematodes, small unsegmented worms, and tardigrades (eight-legged arthropods) are the most common components of microfauna. Many inhabit water films or pore spaces in leaf litter and in the soil, feeding on smaller microorganisms that decompose organic material.

NEKTON

The assemblage of pelagic animals that swim freely, independent of water motion or wind, is called nekton. Only three phyla are represented by adult forms. Chordate nekton include numerous species of bony fishes, the cartilaginous fishes such as the sharks, several species of reptiles (turtles, snakes, and saltwater crocodiles), and mammals such as the whales, porpoises, and seals. Molluscan nekton include the squids and octopods. The only arthropod nekton are decapods, including shrimps, crabs, and lobsters.

Herbivorous nekton are not very common, although a few nearshore and shallow-water species subsist by grazing on plants. Of the nektonic feeding types, zooplankton feeders are the most abundant and include, in addition to many bony fishes, such as the sardines and mackerel, some of the largest nekton, the baleen whales. The molluscans, sharks, and many of the larger bony fishes consume animals bigger than zooplankton. Other fishes and most of the crustaceans are scavengers.

Nektonic species are limited in their areal and vertical distributions by the barriers of temperature, salinity, nutrient supply, and type of sea bottom. The number of nektonic species and individuals decreases with increasing depth in the ocean.

NEUSTON

Neuston is a group of organisms found on top of or attached to the underside of the surface film of water. The neuston includes insects such as whirligig beetles and water striders, some spiders and protozoans, and occasional worms, snails, insect larvae, and hydras. It is distinguished from the plankton, which only incidentally becomes associated with the surface film.

PHYTOPLANKTON

The chief components of marine phytoplankton are found within the algal groups and include diatoms, dinoflagellates and coccolithophorids. Silicoflagellates, cryptomonads, and green algae are found in most plankton samples. Freshwater phytoplankton, usually rich in green algae, also includes diatoms, blue-green algae, and true flagellates.

PLANKTON

Plankton are marine and freshwater organisms, which, because they are nonmotile or because they are too small or too weak to swim against the current, exist in a drifting, floating state. The term plankton is a collective name for all such organisms and includes certain algae, bacteria, protozoans, crustaceans, mollusks, and coelenterates, as well as representatives from almost every other phylum of animals. Plankton is distinguished from nekton, which is composed of strong-swimming animals, and from benthos, which include sessile, creeping, and burrowing organisms on the seafloor. Large floating seaweeds (for example, *Sargassum,* which constitutes the Sargasso Sea) and various related multicellular algae are not considered plankton but pleuston. Organisms resting or swimming on the surface film of the water are called neuston (e.g., the alga *Ochromonas*).

Plankton is the productive base of both marine and freshwater ecosystems, providing food for larger animals and, indirectly, for humans, whose fisheries depend upon plankton. The productivity of an area is dependent upon the availability of nutrients and water-stability conditions. Currents that flow near continents are important to plankton production in an area. The California Current (a continuation of the Kuroshio Drift from Japan) causes an outland transport of water and combines with a compensating nutrient-rich current along the coast of California to make this area highly productive. The same situation exists along the west coast of southern Africa, which is influenced by the Benguela Current, and off the west coast of South America, influenced by the Peru Current.

In the sea an adequate supply of nutrients, including carbon dioxide, enables phytoplankton and benthic algae to transform the light energy of the Sun into energy-rich chemical components through photosynthesis. The bottom-dwelling algae are responsible for about 2 percent of the primary production in the ocean; the remaining 98 percent is attributable to phytoplankton. Most of the phytoplankton serves as food for zooplankton, but some of it is carried below the light zone. After death, this phytoplankton undergoes chemical mineralization, bacterial breakdown, or transformation into sediments. Phytoplankton production usually is greatest from 5 to 10 m below the surface of the water. High light intensity and the lack of nutrient in the regions above a depth of 5 m may be the causes for suboptimal photosynthesis. Although bacteria are found at all depths, they are most abundant either immediately below great phytoplankton populations or just above the bottom.

As a human resource, plankton has only begun to be developed and exploited. It may in time be the chief food supply of the world, in view of its high biological productivity and wide extent. It has been demonstrated on several occasions that large-scale cultures of algae are technically feasible. The unicellular green alga *Chorella* has been used particularly in this connection. Through ample culture conditions, production is directed toward protein content greater than 50 percent. Although this protein has a suitable balance of essential amino acids, its low degree of digestibility prevents practical use. Phytoplankton may become increasingly important in space travel as a source for food and for gas exchange. The carbon dioxide released during respiration of spacecraft personnel would be transformed into organic substances by the algae, while the oxygen liberated during this process would support human respiration.

SCAVENGERS

Scavengers, or carrion-feeders, are animals that feed partly or wholly on the bodies of dead animals. Many invertebrates, such as carrion beetles, live almost entirely on decomposing animal matter. The burying beetles actually enter the dead bodies of small animals before feeding on them underground.

Among vertebrates there are species such as the vultures that exist solely on carrion. Most vertebrates show more flexibility. The bald eagle will scavenge dead fish whenever possible, but it hunts when necessary and will rob the kill of an osprey. Most large mammalian predators, e.g., the lion and the wolf, will opportunistically eat of a carcass killed by another animal. The spotted hyena, widely known as a scavenger, has heavy jaws equipped for crushing bones. Lone hyenas live mostly on carrion, but where large populations exist they form packs and hunt by night. A clan of 30 hyenas may drive off a small group of lions and steal their kill.

SOIL ORGANISMS

Soil organisms are described as any organism inhabiting the soil during part or all of its life. Soil organisms, which range in size from microscopic cells that digest decaying organic material to small mammals that live primarily on other soil organisms, play an important role in maintaining fertility, structure, drainage, and aeration of soil. They also break down plant and animal tissues, releasing stored nutrients and converting them into forms usable by plants. Some soil organisms are pests. Among the soil organisms that are pests of crops are nematodes, slugs and snails, symphylids, beetle larvae, fly larvae, caterpillars, and root aphids. Some soil organisms cause rots, some release substances that inhibit plant growth, and others are hosts for organisms that cause animal diseases.

Since most of the functions of soil organisms are beneficial, earth with large numbers of organisms in it tends to be fertile; one square metre of rich soil can harbour as many as 1 billion organisms.

Soil organisms are commonly divided into five arbitrary groups according to size, the smallest of which are the protists—including bacteria, actinomycetes, and algae. Next are the microfauna, which are less than 100 microns in length and generally feed upon other microorganisms. The microfauna include single-celled protozoans, some smaller flatworms, nematodes, rotifers, and tardigrades (eight-legged invertebrates). The mesofauna are somewhat larger and are heterogeneous, including creatures that feed on microorganisms, decaying matter, and living plants. The category includes nematodes, mites, springtails (wingless insects so called for the springing organ which enables them to leap), the insectlike proturans, which feed on fungi, and the pauropods.

The fourth group, the macrofauna, are also quite diverse. The most common example is the potworm, a white, segmented worm that feeds on fungi, bacteria, and decaying plant material. The group also includes slugs, snails, and millipedes, which feed on plants, and centipedes, beetles and their larvae, and the larvae of flies, which feed on other organisms or on decaying matter.

Megafauna constitute the largest soil organisms and include the largest earthworms, perhaps the most important creatures that live in the topsoil. Earthworms pass both soil and organic matter through their guts, in the process aerating the soil, breaking up the litter of organic material on its surface, and moving material vertically from the surface to the subsoil. This is extremely important to soil fertility, and it develops the structure of the soil as a matrix for plants and other organisms. It has been estimated that earthworms completely turn over the equivalent of all the soil on the planet to a depth one inch (2.5 cm) every 10 years. Some vertebrates are also in the megafauna category; these include all sorts of burrowing animals, such as snakes, lizards, gophers, badgers, rabbits, hares, mice, and moles.

One of the most important roles of soil organisms is breaking up the complex substances in decaying plants and animals so that they can be used again by living plants. This involves soil organisms as catalysts in a number of natural cycles, among the most prominent being the carbon, nitrogen, and sulfur cycles.

The carbon cycle begins in plants, which combine carbon dioxide from the atmosphere with water to make plant tissues such as leaves, stems, and fruits. Animals eat the plants and convert the tissues into animal tissues. The cycle is completed when the animals die and their decaying tissues are eaten by soil organisms, a process that releases carbon dioxide.

Proteins are the basic stuff of organic tissues, and nitrogen is an essential element of all proteins. The availability of nitrogen in forms that plants can use is a basic determinant of the fertility of soils; the role of soil organisms in facilitating the nitrogen cycle is therefore of great importance. When a plant or animal dies, soil organisms break up the complex proteins, polypeptides, and nucleic acids in their bodies and produce ammonium, ions, nitrates, and nitrites that plants then use to build their body tissues.

Both bacteria and blue-green algae can fix nitrogen directly from the atmosphere, but this is less vital to plant development than the symbiotic relationship between the bacteria genus *Rhizobium* and leguminous plants and certain trees and shrubs. In return for secretions from their host that encourage their growth and multiplication, *Rhizobia* fix nitrogen in nodules of the host plant's roots, providing nitrogen in a form usable by the plant.

Soil organisms also participate in the sulfur cycle, mostly by breaking up the naturally abundant sulfur compounds in the soil so that this vital element is available to plants. The smell of rotten eggs so common in swamps and marshes is due to the hydrogen sulfide produced by these microorganisms.

Though soil organisms have become less important in agriculture due to the development of synthetic fertilizers, they play a vital role in woodlands, especially in the creation of humus, a finely separated complex of organic materials composed of decaying leaves and other vegetable matter.

When a leaf falls it cannot be eaten by most animals. After the water-soluble components of the leaf are leached out, fungi and other microflora attack its structure, making it soft and pliable. Now the litter is palatable to a wide variety of invertebrates, which fragment it into a mulch. The multipedes, wood lice, fly larvae, springtails, and earthworms leave the litter relatively unchanged organically, but they create a suitable substrate for the growth of the primary decomposers that break it into simpler chemical compounds. There is also a group called secondary decomposers (some creatures, such as the springtails, are in both groups), which break it down even further.

So the organic matter of leaves is constantly being digested and redigested by waves of increasingly smaller organisms. Eventually the humic substance that remains may be as little as one-fourth of the original organic matter of the litter. Gradually this humus is mixed into the soil by burrowing animals (such as moles, rabbits, etc.) and by the action of the earthworms.

Though some soil organisms can become pests — especially when a single crop is grown repeatedly in the same field, encouraging the proliferation of organisms that prey on their roots — by and large they are essential elements in the process of life, death, and decay, which rejuvenates the environment.

TROPHIC LEVELS

Trophic levels are steps in a nutritive series, or food chain, of an ecosystem. The organisms of a chain are classified into these levels on the basis of their feeding behaviour. The first and lowest level contains the producers, green plants. The plants or their products are consumed by the second-level organisms — the herbivores, or plant eaters. At the third level, primary carnivores, or meat eaters, eat the herbivores; and at the fourth level, secondary carnivores eat the primary carnivores. These categories are not strictly defined, as many organisms feed on several trophic levels; for example, some carnivores also consume plant materials or carrion and are called omnivores, and some herbivores occasionally consume animal matter. A separate trophic level, the decomposers or transformers, consists of organisms such as bacteria and fungi that break down dead organisms and waste materials into nutrients usable by the producers.

ZOOPLANKTON

The animal-like community of plankton is known as zooplankton, which is further divided into two groups. Temporary plankton consists of planktonic eggs and larvae of members of the benthos and nekton; permanent plankton includes all animals that live their complete life cycles in a floating state. The temporary plankton, particularly abundant in coastal areas, is characteristically seasonal in occurrence, though variations in spawning time of different species ensure its presence in all seasons. Representatives from nearly every phylum of the animal kingdom are found in the permanent plankton. Among the protozoans, planktonic foraminiferans and radiolarians are so abundant and widespread that their skeletons constitute the bulk of bottom sediments over wide ocean areas. They are absent in fresh water. The ciliate protozoans are represented mainly by the tintinnids, which are between 20 and 640 microns in size and sometimes occur in vast numbers. Among the planktonic coelenterates are the beautiful siphonophores (e.g., *Physalia*, the Portuguese man-of-war) and the jellyfishes. Planktonic ctenophores, called comb jellies, or sea walnuts, are also common. Freshwater rotifers may be present in plankton in vast numbers during the warmer seasons. A group of organisms that can be found at all latitudes, both in surface water and at great depths, are the marine arrowworms (e.g., *Sagitta*), important planktonic predators. Oysters, mussels, other marine bivalves, and snails begin life as planktonic larvae. The wing snails (Pteropoda) spend their entire life cycles as plankton.

Crustaceans are the most important members of the zooplankton. They are the marine counterparts of insects on land; on land, as in the sea, the arthropods are the most diverse and numerous of all animal phyla. The copepod

Calanus finmarchicus is important as food for the herring, and the euphausiid *Euphausia superba,* commonly known as krill, is the main food source for blue and fin whales in the Antarctic Ocean. These whales, particularly blue and finback whales, migrate to waters where spawning of these crustaceans occurs; and the rapid growth of these large mammals, feeding entirely on plankton, is impressive.

There is a pronounced tendency for zooplankton to perform diurnal vertical migrations in both lakes and the sea. This migratory behaviour varies with stages in the life cycle, seasons of the year, latitude, hydrographic structure, and meteorological conditions. Generally, the animals ascend toward the surface at sunset from daytime depths. At midnight, if there is no optical stimulus (e.g., moon, artificial light), some of the animals return to the daytime depths, then approach the surface once again just before dawn. As the sun rises, all descend to their daytime level.

GLOSSARY

abiotic Term used to describe the nonliving parts of an ecosystem.

autotroph An organism that serves as a primary producer in a food chain.

benthos The sea biota that dwells on or near the ocean floor.

biodiversity In general, the variety of life found within an ecosystem or, more typically, the total variety of life on Earth.

biogeography The study of the distribution of animals and plants.

biomass A term used to refer to the weight of all the biota in an area.

biome The largest geographic biotic unit, a major community of plants and animals with similar life forms and environmental conditions.

biosphere The thin, life-supporting stratum of Earth's surface.

biota The collective name for the living organisms—plants and animals—on Earth.

coniferous Term used to describe trees that bear seeds in cones and have needles or flat leaves.

cyanobacteria Another name for the blue-green algae.

deciduous Term used to describe trees in temperate forests that have broad, flat leaves.

detritivore Animals and plants that feed on the decaying organic matter.

ecosystem A grouping of biota, their physical environment, and all their interrelationships within a particular unit of space.

ectotherm An animal that regulates its body temperature based on external sources such as sunlight or a heated rock surface.

ecotone A transition area of vegetation between two different plant communities.

endemism Term referring to the quality or state of being found in a particular area; being biologically indigenous to an area.

endotherm An animal whose body temperature is regulated independent of its environment.

estivation A form of torpor experienced by animals in response to heat stress.

estuary A partly enclosed coastal body of water composed of mixed river water and seawater.

fen A type of low-lying bog; an area of land wholly or partly covered with water and dominated by grasses and grasslike plants.

gaia hypothesis The model of the Earth in which its living and nonliving parts are viewed as a complex interacting system that can be thought of as a single organism.

heterotroph An organism that consumes other organisms within a food chain.

lacustrine A term used to define lake ecosystems.

nekton Groups of organisms that swim in the pelagic, or upper, portion of the world's oceans independent of waves or wind.

pelagic zone The ecological realm that includes the entire ocean water column.

scree An area of rock debris that has accumulated at the base of a mountain cliff.

tree line The region of transition in mountain ecosystems or between boreal and tundra ecosystems where trees get smaller and the space between them gets larger.

tundra An ecosystem defined by great expanses of treeless ground and a harsh, frigid climate.

BIBLIOGRAPHY

THE BIOSPHERE

Mitchell B. Rambler, Lynn Margulis, and René Fester (eds.), *Global Ecology: Towards a Science of the Biosphere* (1989), describes and interprets the biosphere and the processes that occur within it. Richard J. Huggett, *Climate, Earth Processes, and Earth History* (1991), discusses the changing of the biosphere over time. William K. Purves, Gordon H. Orians, and H. Craig Heller, *Life: The Science of Biology*, 4th ed. (1994), treats such topics as general ecology, the biosphere, and the origin of life. Paul R. Ehrlich and Jonathan Roughgarden, *The Science of Ecology* (1987), describes organisms in their environments. Lawrence E. Joseph, *Gaia: The Growth of an Idea* (1990), is a simple explanation of the Gaia hypothesis. Leslie A. Real and James H. Brown (eds.), *Foundations of Ecology: Classic Papers with Commentaries* (1991), provides a historical perspective of the major issues in ecology. Lynn Margulis and Lorraine Olendzenski (eds.), *Environmental Evolution* (1992), discusses the interaction of life and the abiotic components of the Earth, as well as the evolution of life as a consequence of changes to the biosphere over time.

Michael Begon, John L. Harper, and Colin R. Townsend, *Ecology: Individuals, Populations, and Communities*, 2nd ed. (1990); Robert E. Ricklefs, *Ecology*, 3rd ed. (1990); Charles J. Krebs, *Ecology: The Experimental Analysis of Distribution and Abundance*, 4th ed. (1994); and the work by Ehrlich and Roughgarden, cited above, are well-written textbooks that provide good general descriptions of energy flow and nutrient cycling through ecosystems, population biology, and community ecology.

D.L. DeAngelis, *Dynamics of Nutrient Cycling and Food Webs* (1992), is a mathematical treatment of the rates of energy flow and nutrient cycling through ecosystems. An in-depth treatment of how the major nutrients necessary for plant growth move in cycles between plants and the soil can be found in F.J. Stevenson, *Cycles of Soil: Carbon, Nitrogen, Phosphorus, Sulfur, Micronutrients* (1986). A review of the groups of microorganisms and their various roles in the nitrogen cycle is Janet I. Sprent and Peter Sprent, *Nitrogen Fixing Organisms: Pure and Applied Aspects* (1990).

David A. Dunnette and Robert J. O'Brien (eds.), *The Science of Global Change: The Impact of Human Activities on the Environment* (1992), reports on the ways in which human activities are influencing biogeochemical cycles and climate change. Robert L. Peters and Thomas E. Lovejoy (eds.), *Global Warming and Biological Diversity* (1992); and Peter M. Kareiva, Joel G. Kingsolver, and Raymond B. Huey (eds.), *Biotic Interactions and Global Change* (1993), investigate how human-induced global changes affect organisms, population, species, communities, and ecosystems.

BIOMES AND BIOGEOGRAPHIC REGIONS

León Croizat, *Panbiogeography; or, An Introductory Synthesis of Zoogeography, Phytogeography, and Geology; with notes on evolution, systematics, ecology, anthropology, etc.*, 2 vol. in 3 (1958), is dated but must still be admired for its incredible scope and breadth of learning, and his *Space, Time, Form: The Biological Synthesis* (1962), discusses various topics, including evolution, biology, and biogeography. R. Hengeveld, *Dynamic Biogeography* (1990), surveys biogeographic methods such as taxonomic clustering techniques, ecological adaptations, species richness estimation, and areography. D.R. Stoddart, *On Geography and Its History* (1986), is a scholarly yet easily read text on geography and its impact on biology. Gareth Nelson and Don E. Rosen (eds.), *Vicariance Biogeography: A Critique* (1981), explains the basic principles of the vicariance school.

J.C. Briggs, *Biogeography and Plate Tectonics* (1987), is a region-by-region account of the distribution of plants and animals in the context of geologic history. Philip Jackson Darlington, *Zoogeography: The Geographic Distribution of Animals* (1957, reprinted 1982), although dated, may still be regarded as the definitive statement on historical zoogeography. Joachim Illies, *Introduction to Zoogeography*, trans. from German (1974); and Paul Müller, *Aspects of Zoogeography* (1974), two introductory texts, summarize both historical zoogeography and biotic regions. George Gaylord Simpson, *Splendid Isolation: The Curious History of South American Mammals* (1980), explores the origin and evolution of the mammals on this continent.

THE MOUNTAIN ECOSYSTEM

Larry W. Price, *Mountains & Man: A Study of Process and Environment* (1981), provides a broad treatment of the mountain lands of the world. W. Tranquillini, *Physiological Ecology of the Alpine Timberline: Tree Existence at High Altitudes with Special Reference to the European Alps* (1979), details the Alpine tree line ecology using international examples, with particular reference to temperate-zone mountains. François Vuilleumier and Maximina Monasterio (eds.), *High Altitude Tropical Biogeography* (1986), discusses equatorial high mountain flora and fauna.

THE POLAR ECOSYSTEM

Peter J. Marchand, *Life in the Cold: An Introduction to Winter Ecology*, 2nd ed. (1991), describes the adaptations of plants and animals to the physical constraints of temperature, snow, and wind in high-latitude environments. Sanford Moss, *Natural History of the Antarctic Peninsula* (1988), an illustrated text, provides general descriptions of the life-forms of the Antarctic Peninsula in relation to the climate and adjacent marine system. G.E. Fogg, *A History of Antarctic Science* (1992), comprehensively reviews research done in Antarctica. Jack D. Ives and Roger G. Barry (eds.), *Arctic and Alpine Environments* (1974), looks at these eco-systems, their physical components, adaptations of life-forms present (including humans and their prehistori-cal and historical presence), and the impact of technology on these environments. *Antarctic Bibliography* (annual); and *Arctic Bibliography*, 16 vol. (1953–75), are useful refer-ence works for publications on these regions.

E. Imre Friedmann and Roseli Ocampo, "Endolithic Blue-Green Algae in the Dry Valleys: Primary Producers in the Antarctic Desert Ecosystem," *Science*, 193(4259):1247–1249 (Sept. 24, 1976), details the unique forms of life found within rocks in Antarctica. Larry L. Tieszen (ed.), *Vegetation and Production Ecology of an Alaskan Arctic Tundra* (1978), focuses on the vegetation and its primary production in a wet tundra ecosystem. George O. Batzli (ed.), *Patterns of Vegetation and Herbivory in Arctic Tundra* (1980), describes the vegetation as well as the role of herbivores in the ecol-ogy of the tundra. George A. Llano (ed.), *Adaptations Within Antarctic Ecosystems* (1977), symposium proceed-ings, looks at the adaptation of organisms in both marine and terrestrial ecosystems. N. Leader-Williams, *Reindeer on South Georgia: The Ecology of an Introduced Population* (1988), discusses the effects of introducing mammals to the southern islands. L.C. Bliss (ed.), *Truelove Lowland, Devon Island, Canada: A High Arctic Ecosystem* (1977), focuses on ecosystem components. Yu.I. Chernov (IU.I. Chernov), *The Living Tundra* (1985; originally published in Russian,

1980), is a classic description of tundra landscapes, ecosystems, and plant and animal components. Jerry Brown et al. (eds.), *An Arctic Ecosystem: The Coastal Tundra at Barrow, Alaska* (1980), compiles research findings on ecosystem components of the Arctic tundra. L.C. Bliss, O.W. Heal, and J.J. Moore (eds.), *Tundra Ecosystems: A Comparative Analysis* (1981), is an excellent comprehensive synthesis on circumpolar and tundra systems. F. Stuart Chapin III et al. (eds.), *Arctic Ecosystems in a Changing Climate: An Ecophysiological Perspective* (1992), describes the physiological processes of plants and animals in this region and also discusses the consequences of global climate change on these processes.

THE MARINE ECOSYSTEM

A general description of the ecology of marine life can be found in R.S.K. Barnes and R.N. Hughes, *An Introduction to Marine Ecology*, 2nd ed. (1988). K.H. Mann and J.R.N. Lazier, *Dynamics of Marine Ecosystems: Biological-Physical Interactions in the Ocean* (1991), discusses oceanographic phenomena on a variety of spatial scales and their relevance to marine animals. Life in the sea is examined in James L. Sumich, *An Introduction to the Biology of Marine Life*, 5th ed. (1992); and Richard A. Davis, Jr., *Oceanography: An Introduction to the Marine Environment*, 2nd ed. (1991), which also treats the nature of different marine environments. John Mauchline and Tokahisa Nemoto (eds.), *Marine Biology: Its Accomplishment and Future Prospect* (1991), covers such topics as marine physiology and ecosystems, benthos and the impact of pollutants, phytoplankton studies, and polar seas. Richard S. Boardman, Alan H. Cheetham, and Albert J. Rowell (eds.), *Fossil Invertebrates* (1987), describes fossil invertebrate taxonomy in detail and gives an account of the geologic age of environments in which fossils were found. Richard C. Brusca and Gary J. Brusca, *Invertebrates* (1990), reviews the taxonomy of both marine and terrestrial invertebrates.

Karl F. Lagler et al., *Ichthyology*, 2nd ed. (1977), is a general text. Harold C. Bold and Michael J. Wynne, *Introduction to the Algae: Structure and Reproduction*, 2nd ed. (1985), discusses the distribution, reproduction, cultivation, classification, and fossil record of algae. E.B. Sherr and B.F. Sherr, "Planktonic Microbes: Tiny Cells at the Base of the Ocean's Food Webs," *Trends in Ecology & Evolution*, 6(2):50–54 (1991), reviews the role of microbes in the ocean. John D. Gage and Paul A. Tyler, *Deep-Sea Biology: A Natural History of Organisms at the Deep-Sea Floor* (1991), looks at organisms of the deep sea and deep-sea vents. M.J. Kingsford, "Biotic and Abiotic Structure in the Pelagic Environment: Importance to Small Fishes," *Bulletin of Marine Science*, 53(2):393–415 (1993), examines such structures as marine snow and drifting algae, among other topics. R. Robin Baker (ed.), *Fantastic Journeys: The Marvels of Animal Migration* (1991), traces the migrations of aquatic and terrestrial animals. J.A. Gulland (ed.), *Fish Population Dynamics: The Implications for Management*, 2nd ed. (1988), contains studies on fisheries of the world and why populations vary.

THE BOUNDARY ECOSYSTEM

Donald S. McLusky, *The Estuarine Ecosystem,* 2nd ed. (1989), is a concise account of the subject at the college level. John W. Day, Jr., et al., *Estuarine Ecology* (1989), deals with physical aspects, plants, animals, organic detritus, and human impacts, including some information on lagoons. K.H. Mann, *Ecology of Coastal Waters: A Systems Approach* (1982), discusses estuaries as well as sea grass, marsh grass, mangrove, seaweed, and mudflat communities. S.P. Long and C.F. Mason, *Saltmarsh Ecology* (1983), treats such topics as the formation, flora, fauna, physiography, and conservation of salt marshes. J.R. Lewis, *The Ecology of Rocky Shores* (1964), is still a standard work on organisms and their relationship to the environment. Roger N. Brehaut, *Ecology of Rocky Shores* (1982), is a concise, nontechnical text with suggestions for further reading. A.C. Brown and A. McLachlan, *Ecology of Sandy Shores* (1990), discusses sandy beaches worldwide. John R. Clark, *Coastal Ecosystems: Ecological Considerations for Management of the Coastal Zone* (1974), and *Coastal Ecosystem Management: A Technical Manual for the Conservation of Coastal Zone Resources* (1977, reprinted 1983), discuss the ecology of marine boundary ecosystems and the problems of management.

Patrick Dugan (ed.), *Wetlands in Danger: A World Conservation Atlas* (1993), summarizes all the world's major wetlands and wetland types. William J. Mitsch and James G. Gosselink, *Wetlands*, 2nd ed. (1993), describes seven major types of wetlands and the principles common to all wetlands. William A. Niering, *Wetlands* (1985), an illustrated text, details the habitats' features and characteristics. William J. Mitsch (ed.), *Global Wetlands: Old World and New* (1994), covers topics such as the biogeochemistry, modeling, and ecological engineering of wetlands, as well as wildlife management and river delta management. Regional accounts can be found in Canada Committee on Ecological (Biophysical) Land Classification, National Wetlands Working Group, *Wetlands of Canada* (1988), including an extensive bibliography; A.J. McComb and P.S. Lake, *Australian Wetlands* (1990); and Bates Littlehales and William A. Niering, *Wetlands of North America* (1991), both heavily illustrated with photographs. Edward Maltby,

Waterlogged Wealth: Why Waste the World's Wet Places? (1986), describes the functions of wetlands and the degree to which they are threatened around the world. Jon A. Kusler, William J. Mitsch, and Joseph S. Larson, "Wetlands," *Scientific American*, 270(1):64–70 (January 1994), summarizes the structure and function of wetlands, emphasizing the importance of a fluctuating water level on ecosystem function. Dennis Whigham, Dagmar Dykyjová, and Slavomil Hejný (eds.), *Wetlands of the World: Inventory, Ecology, and Management* (1993–), is a scholarly treatment. Max Finlayson and Michael Moser (eds.), *Wetlands* (1991), deals with all inland waters of the world from a conservation perspective.

INDEX

DATE DUE